D1030660

LOOK
AT A
FLOWER

LOOK
AT A FLOWER

by Anne Ophelia T. Dowden

Illustrated by the Author

THOMAS Y. CROWELL COMPANY   NEW YORK

ACKNOWLEDGMENTS   In collecting the hundreds of specimens on which these drawings are based, I often had to turn for help to friends throughout the country, and I am deeply indebted to all of them for their interest and effort.

In the preparation of the text, I received generous and scholarly assistance from many people, to whom I can only offer grateful thanks: to Mr. John C. Pallister, research associate in entomology at the American Museum of Natural History, who read the manuscript and gave many helpful suggestions; to Miss Elizabeth Hall, Sarah Gildersleeve Fife librarian at the New York Botanical Garden, who guided me to sources of research; to Dr. Gordon Alexander, professor of biology at the University of Colorado, who made a most precise critique of the manuscript; to Mr. Joseph Monachino, herbarium custodian of the New York Botanical Garden, who read the several drafts of the text with a discerning professional eye; to Mr. George A. Kalmbacher, taxonomist at the Brooklyn Botanic Garden, who supplied plants and botanical information and friendly encouragement, and who gave endless time to scrutinizing text and drawings; to my husband, Raymond B. Dowden, who helped in an infinite number of ways, from plant collecting to manuscript reading, and even to bathing among buttercups and daisies when the demands of the blooming season kept the bathtub full of specimens.

A. O. T. D.

INTRODUCTION

Nearly everyone is interested to some extent in the flowers that grow around him; and, though many people are probably satisfied when they have learned to tell a rose from a buttercup, those who really love plants soon see more than the pretty posy and become aware of beautiful and significant structures within it.

These structures are not accidental embellishments. They are all part of the intricate machinery of pollination and seed-making. Anyone who will spend a few hours watching a blossom will discover things about its life-relationships that should amaze and delight him.

The story of these activities is often a complicated one; but, in the presentation of it here, every effort has been made to keep it as simple and general as possible. All the plants illustrated or referred to in the text, with two or three exceptions, are common in American fields or gardens, and all flowers and floral details have been drawn from living specimens. Insect studies have been made chiefly from preserved specimens.

Though this volume can be used as a foundation for serious botanical study, its purpose is achieved if it stimulates the reader into his own investigations and directs him to friendships with living plants in their everyday surroundings. It is intended as a guide to plant watching and an introduction to the tiny floral arenas where things are always happening. And it should lead both student and dabbler beyond the larger shapes of a flower into the wonder of form and the beauty of design in its small and often hidden parts.

CONTENTS

BEARBERRY

WHY ARE PLANTS CLASSIFIED?

Naming plants began in prehistoric times. Early man had to know which ones he could eat and which provided wood for burning and for building shelters. As time went on, he found that some would cure his ailments. He learned all this by experiment; and, in order to hand on what he had discovered, he had to tell about and describe these herbs and trees. This was the start of the naming of plants and the science of botany.

By the time of the Greeks, plant lore had become so important that the first true botanists appeared. By then, plants were used for all kinds of things—food, clothing, shelter, oils, dyes. Because one of the most important uses was in medicine, the doctors became the botanists. For the preparation of their drugs, they had to study plants. As they accumulated more and more information, they had to put it in some kind of order so that they could use it easily. Thus they made the first botanical *classifications,* or orderly groupings, all based on the medicinal qualities of plants.

1

Over the centuries, the growth of botanical knowledge has changed these early classifications. Now we know more about plant structures and the meaning of those structures. Even more important, we know that plants have been evolving for millions of years. The ones growing around us today are the descendants of ancient forms, most of which have disappeared.

Through many thousands of generations, plants have changed in innumerable ways. Tracing these changes is the only means we have of discovering lines of descent. Following the lines of descent (like studying the family trees of people) is interesting in itself. But it is more than interesting; it is important, because it explains the characteristics and relationships of present-day plants.

Often tracing the ancestry of a plant is difficult. Many steps in the evolutionary process—the so-called "missing links"—have disappeared. We will probably never be sure of the origin of all plants. But study continues, and new discoveries are being made all the time.

When botanists classify a flower today, they are in a sense trying to reveal the actual plan of nature. They are explaining the relationship of that plant to all the other plants in the world. They are introducing it, with its sisters and its cousins and its aunts.

The introduction will be in Latin and Latinized Greek. Common names of plants vary from place to place and are therefore not accurate. But Latin names are universal and reliable. They can be recognized on the pages of an English or a German or a Hebrew book—or even in a column of Chinese characters.

Latin names seem hard only because they are unfamiliar.

Each name means something and often tells us about the appearance or use of the plant. For example, the common wild geranium or crane's-bill is called by botanists *Geranium maculatum*. "Geranium" comes from a Greek word meaning "crane," because of the pointed beak that tops the plant's seed capsule. "Maculatum" is Latin for "spotted."

Every plant has this kind of double name, which indicates the *genus* and *species* the plant belongs to. A species (plural *species*) is the basic unit of classification. It is a group of plants or animals which all have in common certain distinctive characteristics. A genus (plural *genera*) is a group of closely related species.

The common dandelion is called *Taraxacum officinale*. (The word "officinale" means "of the shops" and tells us that this plant used to be sold as a medicine.) This double name indicates that the dandelion belongs to the genus *Taraxacum* and to the species *officinale*. No other plant on earth is entitled to that name. There are other kinds of dandelions in the genus *Taraxacum*—*Taraxacum laevigatum*, for instance. But the common kind that is a pest in our gardens is always *Taraxacum officinale*.

These dandelions have close relatives, such as chicory and daisy, which are much like them, but not enough like them to belong to the same genus. Chicory belongs to the genus *Cichorium*, daisy to the genus *Chrysanthemum*. But all three genera are included in the same family—the Compositae.

From that we go on into larger and larger groupings. The Composite family is grouped with other families in the order Campanulales. This order belongs, with other orders, in the subclass Metachlamydeae.

Classifying a plant is like addressing a person. He has two names, he lives in a certain house, on a certain street, in a certain town, in a certain county, in a certain state, in the United States of America. Anyone who knows all this about him can find him very easily. In the same way, classification puts into orderly arrangement all the things we know about a plant.

The "address" or classification of our dandelion would look like this:

Species—*officinale*
Genus—*Taraxacum*
Family—Compositae
Order—Campanulales
Subclass—Metachlamydeae
Class—Dicotyledoneae
Subdivision—Angiospermae
Division—Spermatophyta
Kingdom—Plantae

This seems like a frightening array of long names, and, fortunately, only professional botanists have need for all of them. But species, genera, and families are important even to the beginner. Whenever anyone completely and accurately identifies a plant, he gives its genus and species names. And he often includes the family name too.

Knowing about plant families is as interesting as knowing about human ones. (Think of the Adams family and its part in American history.) The Rose family, for instance, includes not only the glamorous blossoms we call "roses," but also most of our common fruits: apples, cherries, strawberries.

4

Sometimes merely knowing a plant's family is enough. Perhaps we have found an unfamiliar flower. We discover after some study that it is a close relative of the clovers and the beans—a member of the Pea family. We have put it in familiar company, and we are satisfied.

We can often do this simply by looking at it. The flowers and pods of the Pea family have a certain typical structure; the leaves and stems and roots often have characteristics different from those of other plants. We can see most of these things as well as any expert can. And we will understand their importance if we learn how plants are constructed and how they function.

LENTIL

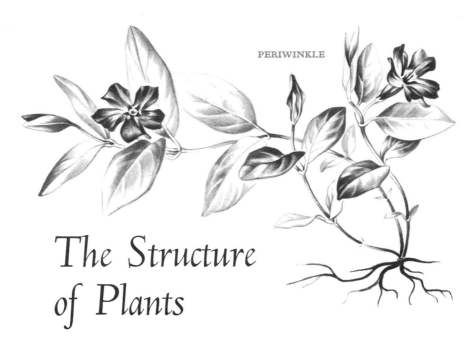

PERIWINKLE

The Structure
of Plants

Plants are constructed in thousands of different patterns—far too many to consider here. We will look at only one group, the flowering plants or Angiosperms (see page 4).

Even this one group includes many patterns. It ranges from giant trees of the tropical jungles to tiny mosslike plants of the Arctic tundra. But each of its members is "built" out of some or all of these basic parts: roots, stems, leaves, and flowers.

However much these parts vary in size and shape and position, the variations have all grown out of some particular need of the plant. They tell us something of its history. They help us to trace its ancestry and to place it in the correct family, genus, and species.

Each part has its special function to perform in nourishing the plant or providing offspring to carry on the species. The ROOTS, underground, serve as anchor and support. From the earth they absorb water and dissolved minerals, and they re-

6

ceive and store food materials which have been manufactured by the upper portions of the plant. They may be delicate and hairlike or thick and fleshy.

STEMS sometimes have underground portions which look like roots: the *bulbs* of onion or tulip, the *rhizomes* of Solomon's-seal, the *tubers* of potatoes. But most often stems stand up above the earth. They support the branches, leaves, and flowers, and act as a conveyor system to carry food materials up and down.

Simple Leaf
CHERRY

LEAVES usually have broad, flat blades spread out to catch the light, which acts on their green chlorophyl to produce the sugar and starch that feeds the plant. Leaves sometimes grow from the stem, sometimes only from the base of the plant; and the way they are arranged on the stem often helps in identification. Leaves may be *simple* (all in one piece), like those of a cherry tree. Or they may be *compound* (divided into small leaflets), like the leaves of a rose or a blackberry.

Compound leaves
ROSE

FLOWERS are the reproductive organs of a plant. They exist solely for the purpose of producing the seeds which will in turn produce new plants.

Seeds usually will not form unless the egg cells of a flower are fertilized. Fertilization means that a male cell, or sperm, joins with a female cell, or egg, and stimulates it to growth. The male cells of a flower are in the pollen manufactured by its stamens. The female cells are contained in another part— the pistil.

BLACKBERRY

An essential step in the production of seeds is the bringing together of pollen cells and egg cells, called *pollination*. This may be accomplished in a number of ways—most often with the help of insects or wind. But, whatever the pollination method, every part of every flower has a shape and position necessary for that method and a share in the process by which the plant reproduces itself.

If we pick a blossom of the common wild geranium or crane's-bill and carefully pull it to pieces, we can see the flower parts in a simple and typical relationship.

In the center of the flower is the PISTIL, the seed-producing organ. It consists of three sections: At its base is the *ovary*, a bag containing the future seeds. At its top is the *stigma*, a knob which will later spread out into five arms to receive pollen. Between these two is a stalk to hold the knob at the proper height—the *style*. Inside the ovary are tiny bodies called *ovules*, which after fertilization will grow into seeds.

Encircling the pistil are the STAMENS, or pollen-producing organs—ten of them in a geranium. The powdery pollen comes out of a little sac—the *anther*. This sac is borne at the end of a delicate, threadlike stalk—the *filament*.

Around the stamens is a ring of five lavender *petals*. These as a group are called the COROLLA, or "little crown." They serve as a banner to attract insects, and they provide the insects with a landing platform. At times they shield the valuable pollen and nectar.

Below the petals lies the outermost ring of parts—the five green *sepals*, which together form the *calyx*. The calyx is primarily a wrap. It encloses and protects the young bud. And later it surrounds the growing ovary, often clinging until long after the seeds are scattered.

These parts form the basic structure of any flower, but they may vary greatly and they are not all present in all flowers. Such variations provide important clues to plant relationships.

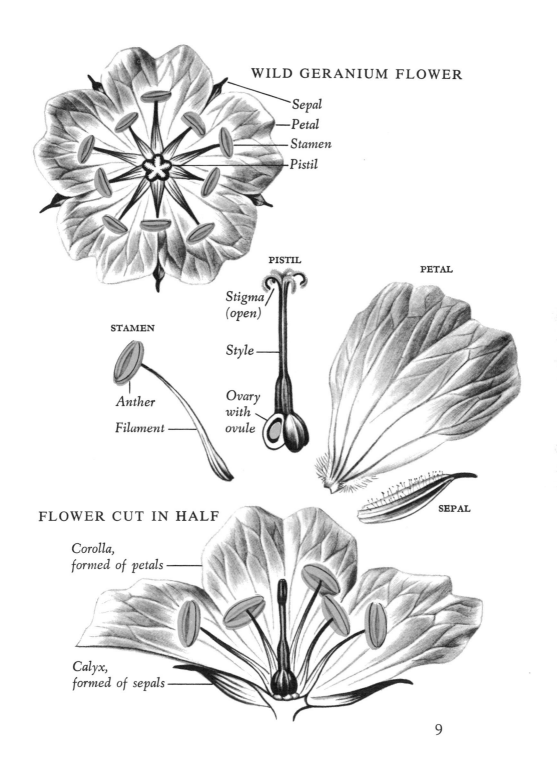

WILD GERANIUM FLOWER

Sepal
Petal
Stamen
Pistil

PISTIL

Stigma
(open)

Style

Ovary
with
ovule

PETAL

STAMEN

Anther

Filament

SEPAL

FLOWER CUT IN HALF

Corolla,
formed of petals

Calyx,
formed of sepals

9

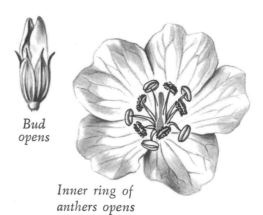

Bud
opens

Inner ring of
anthers opens

Pollination

How the Geranium Produces Seeds

The wild geranium goes about making seeds in a fairly simple way. Its methods will show us something of the methods of all flowering plants.

The carefully arranged steps of fertilization begin as soon as the bud has opened. The filaments, the delicate stalks that bear the anther sacs, swing them out in two rings. Soon the anthers in the inner ring crack open and release their pollen.

This "flower dust" might very easily be smeared on the nearby pistil if that pistil were mature and ready for pollination. But it is not ready. It stands with its stigma tightly closed in the center of the flower and no pollen can reach its sensitive surfaces. This is to prevent the flower's being fertilized by its own pollen, which is bad for the species.

Several hours later, the pollen of the first ring of anthers has almost all been carried off by insects, and the second set of anthers cracks open. By the next morning, most of the pollen

10

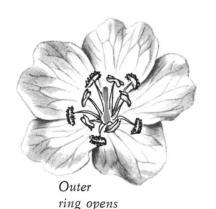

Outer
ring opens

Anthers drop,
stigma opens

Flower shrivels

Sepals fold
around pistil

Style grows
into a beak

is gone. The stamens gradually drop downward and shed their anthers. This leaves the stigma standing alone, well above them. It starts to split from the tip down and opens out into five widespread arms. Each arm is covered with a bristly surface. It is now a *receptive* stigma, waiting for insects to come from other flowers with pollen on their bodies.

Thus, in the normal course of events, a geranium flower's pollen never reaches its own receptive stigma. But occasionally, for some reason, no insect brings the much desired "foreign" pollen, that is, pollen from other plants. Then self pollination may take place. As the flower withers, the stigma arms twist and the petals and filaments crinkle up. At last it is possible for them to touch each other. And at last the stigma can catch the few grains of pollen still lingering in the flower.

A day or two after pollination, the petals and stamens drop off. The stigma shrivels and the sepals fold up around the ovary. The style grows longer and thicker. It now becomes the "beak" which gives the plant the name some people use—crane's-bill.

11

Very few flowers have such a beak. Usually the style dries up and disappears with the stigma as soon as its part in pollination is finished. But the geranium's style remains in place to be used later in seed distribution.

In the meantime, the geranium flower has been pollinated and fertilized. Each pollen grain germinated in the sticky, sugary solution on the stigma. It swelled until it burst its coat. Then it sent a long pollen tube down through the style into the ovary. There the tip of the tube entered one of the ovules and released a tiny sperm cell. This united with the egg cell of an ovule to form a new plant. Each fertilized ovule thus contains one young plant—called an *embryo*—and becomes one seed.

The geranium flower produces five seeds. They ripen for a few weeks in the five capsules at the base of the long beak. When the seeds are mature, beak and capsules split apart. They snap suddenly up and outward, and the seeds go bouncing off in all directions, to form other geranium plants the following year.

Pollen grain

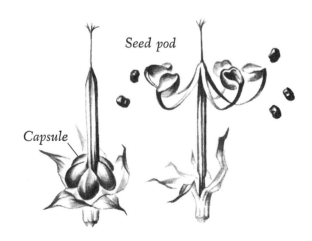

Pollen tube enters ovule

Seed pod

Capsule

12

The Problems of Pollination

The parts of flowers are easy to see. Botanists of a thousand years ago knew them very well, but those botanists could have told us nothing about what the parts are for.

Not until the seventeenth century did scientists discover that pollen must reach the stigma of a flower before fertilization can take place. And still later they learned the ways pollen is transferred and the laws which govern the process.

A flower seldom pollinates itself. It needs the pollen from another flower of the same species. This is called *cross fertilization*. Since the plants themselves cannot move to deliver their pollen to each other, they must have helpers which can move. Such helpers are *pollinizing agents*. They may be wind, water, insects, or small animals like hummingbirds or snails. But wind and insects are by far the most important.

Finally, in the middle of the nineteenth century, botanists discovered why plants should not pollinate themselves. Cross fertilization is the basis of plant evolution, the cause of almost all the variety of today's floral world. It enables plants to improve their heredity and to produce new forms to meet the changes in their environment. Most new forms come about by cross breeding. In this way the heredity of two parent plants is mixed, and the offspring will be different from either parent.

Nature is constantly experimenting, just as the horticulturists are. Some of the new forms she produces will live and thrive and become a permanent part of the plant world. Thus, slowly and over many generations, new species are produced. In the

CLOVER

13

same way, existing species are changed to fit better into their surroundings. It is as though the plant, by trial and error, tries to arrive at the perfect type.

Self fertilization repeats over and over again all characteristics of a species, both good and bad. Though plants do sometimes pollinate themselves, this can be dangerous and at times even disastrous. If the surroundings change, the plant will be unable to change with them.

Self pollination is, therefore, generally undesirable, and plants have developed effective ways of preventing it. Most commonly, the pistils and stamens of each flower mature at different times. Sometimes the stamens ripen first. Then their pollen is gone before the stigma is ready to be fertilized. This happens in a garlic flower just as it did in the wild geranium. On the other hand, some flowers, like lamb's-quarters, put out their pistils ahead of their stamens, and the stigma shrivels before the anthers open. This is especially common among wind-pollinated blossoms.

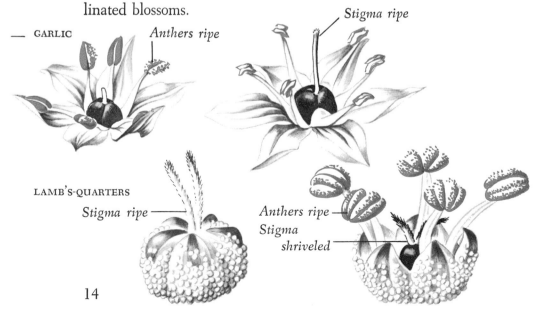

— GARLIC — *Anthers ripe*

Stigma ripe

LAMB'S-QUARTERS

Stigma ripe

Anthers ripe
Stigma shriveled

14

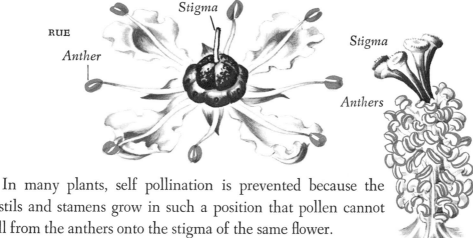

RUE

Stigma

Anther

Stigma

Anthers

HIBISCUS

In many plants, self pollination is prevented because the pistils and stamens grow in such a position that pollen cannot fall from the anthers onto the stigma of the same flower.

In other cases, stamens and pistils change position as the blossom grows older. In a young flower, the stamens often stand out in front of the pistil. They stay there until they have shed their pollen; then they drop aside. The pistil in its turn grows forward into the place where the stamens were. There it opens its receptive stigma and waits for insects. The insect which visits a young flower receives on his body a dab of pollen from the protruding anthers. Then he flies to an older flower. The same part of his body will now touch the stigma and leave some pollen on it.

FIREWEED

Older flower

Young flower

Pistil

Pistil

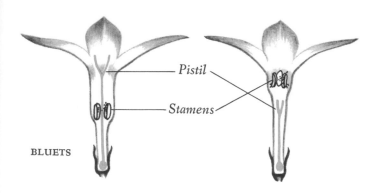

Pistil

Stamens

BLUETS

Still other flowers have pistils and stamens of different lengths which an insect must match to the pistils and stamens of another flower. The tiny bluets produces two kinds of blossoms: one with low stamens and high pistil, the other with low pistil and high stamens. An insect thrusts his tongue into a blossom, and it is smeared with pollen at a certain height. Then, if he flies to another bluets plant, he will find stigmas waiting at exactly the same height. Pollen from high-stamened flowers brushes onto high pistils; pollen from low-stamened flowers is caught by low pistils.

The flowers of purple-loosestrife have pistil-stamen sets of three different lengths. In this species, pollen from the longest stamens fertilizes the longest pistils. Pollen from the medium-length stamens fertilizes the medium-length pistils, and that from the shortest fertilizes the shortest pistils.

PURPLE-
LOOSESTRIFE

Pistil

Pistil

Pistil

16

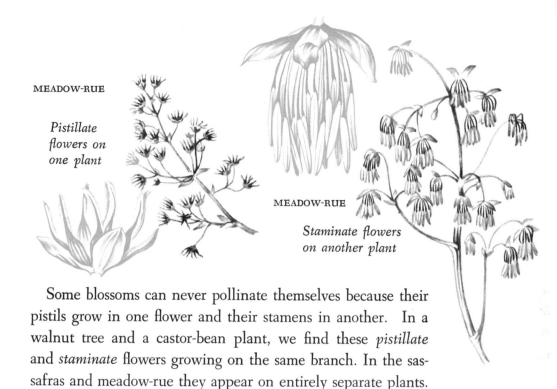

MEADOW-RUE

*Pistillate
flowers on
one plant*

MEADOW-RUE

*Staminate flowers
on another plant*

Some blossoms can never pollinate themselves because their pistils grow in one flower and their stamens in another. In a walnut tree and a castor-bean plant, we find these *pistillate* and *staminate* flowers growing on the same branch. In the sassafras and meadow-rue they appear on entirely separate plants.

There is one more safeguard against self pollination. This has been discovered by laboratory tests. "Foreign" pollen takes precedence over self pollen. Thus, if the pollen of a flower falls on its own stigma at the same time that pollen also comes from another flower, the pollen from the other flower will be the one which takes effect. In some flowers, their own pollen will not germinate at all on their own stigmas.

Sometimes, as we know, a flower's cross pollinating devices fail to work. Then it must, if possible, pollinate itself or produce no seeds. Usually there is some kind of arrangement to take care of this last-minute emergency. Most often, as the blossom dries and shrivels up, its parts touch each other. Then any leftover grains of pollen may finally reach the stigma. The flower, its ovules fertilized just in time, will have seeds.

17

Insect Pollination

Plant races could neither evolve nor survive without the help of pollinizing agents. A botanist has said, "Without bees of all sorts to pollinate their flowers, one hundred thousand species of plants or more would perish from the earth. It seems to me a heavy responsibility for one kind of insect to carry."

Bees are certainly the most important of the pollinators. But other insects also have heavy responsibilities. Many kinds visit blossoms because they like to eat the nectar and pollen they find there. Then they carry pollen on their bodies as they fly from flower to flower.

To attract these insect visitors and to make use of them when they come, flowers have developed an infinite variety of colors and shapes. Each of their parts fits the tongue or body of a particular bee or fly or moth. They gently force the insect into the series of actions necessary for a successful transfer of pollen.

Each species of plant does this in its own particular way. But all insect-flowers possess one or more of these important characteristics: high visibility, scent, nectar, abundant pollen.

A flower is highly visible when it contrasts strongly with its surroundings. Perhaps its intense color glows in the sunshine like a neon light. Perhaps its white petals stand out against dark green foliage or shimmer in the twilight.

18

Color is always a signal to insects, an aid in finding the kind of blossoms they are looking for. Experimenters have proved this by removing the bright petals of certain common bee-flowers. Without the corolla for guidance, the bees always failed to find the nectar and pollen.

We can always be sure that a conspicuous flower is an insect-flower. But sometimes inconspicuous flowers can also attract attention. They may join with others in a cluster. Or they may lure insects with scent or nectar. The fresh odors of rose or violet or carnation were created for insects long before man discovered his own pleasure in their perfume.

Scent is especially useful to night-blooming plants. The heavy and insistent fragrance of honeysuckle and night-blooming-cereus is a far-flung signal to moths. But odors do not have to be sweet to serve this purpose. Some flies will go only where a real stink, like that of skunk-cabbage, reminds them of the rotting flesh on which they lay their eggs.

However, plants do not display their bright colors or broadcast their perfumes just to give pleasure to insects. They are advertising the fact that they have food for sale—nectar and pollen. Pollen is necessary to the life process of a flower; but nectar, or "honey," is produced solely to attract insects. And this food is really for sale, because the visitor must pay for it with service.

Nectar is manufactured by glands, or *nectaries*. Sometimes it collects in drops or as a film around the base of the pistil. Sometimes it is stored in special cups. Insects must not only find it, but find it in such a way that they will rub against the anthers and stigma while doing so. Thus they receive the load of pollen they must carry on to another flower.

19

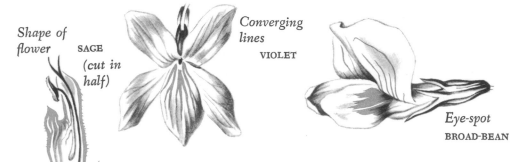

Shape of flower   SAGE *(cut in half)*

Converging lines   VIOLET

Eye-spot   BROAD-BEAN

In most flowers the visitors are directed by markings on the corolla, called *honey-guides*. These may be converging lines, bright eye-spots, rows of dots, or the over-all shape of the corolla itself. Sometimes the cluster of stamens—bright yellow against blue or red or purple petals—is enough to mark the path to the nectar it surrounds.

Some nectaries are simple tiny pockets, like the ones on the petals of a buttercup. Others are little swellings at the base of the pistil. Still others, like those of monkshood, are intricate in shape and sometimes so inaccessible that only certain insects can reach the nectar. This is a way of shutting out undesirable visitors who would not help with pollination.

In the columbine, all five petals are adapted for storing nectar. In nasturtium and jewelweed, a sepal bears the honey spur. In the violet, honey is produced by nectaries on the stamens and stored in a spur on the lowest petal.

Certain flowers have only their pollen with which to woo insect helpers. But pollen is popular too. Honeybees and other insects gather it eagerly. The flower merely produces a large supply, and there is enough to serve both plant and visitors.

Insect anatomy and insect habits vary widely. So an equal

20

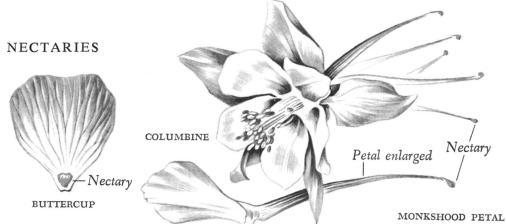

NECTARIES

COLUMBINE

Petal enlarged

Nectary

Nectary

BUTTERCUP

MONKSHOOD PETAL

Nectary

variety has evolved in the shapes of flowers, which are fitted to the needs of their assistants. The size and position of parts— width of throat, depth of nectary, height of anthers—are matched to the measurements of certain insects. By observing those details carefully, we can often guess who the pollinizing agent will be even before we actually meet him.

The Flower and the Insect

Watching pollinizing agents in action is one of the most fascinating entertainments Nature can offer us. Once we have learned to look closely at the remarkable partnership of flower and insect, we will find on every side ingenious devices to amaze and delight us.

But we must not jump to conclusions. It is easy to assume that any insect perched on a certain flower is its pollinizing agent. He can, however, be just sitting there—as casually as he would sit on a fence post. Or he may be a robber, trying to get food for nothing.

Insects which really serve the flowers always have certain characteristics: they must be interested in something the plant

21

has to offer—usually nectar and pollen. They must have mouth parts shaped for eating these substances. They must have furry bodies to which pollen will cling. And they must have wings if they are to travel far enough to distribute pollen widely.

Many insects answer this description. Most important are butterflies, moths, flies, and bees—honeybees, bumblebees, leaf-cutting bees, and many other kinds.

Honeybees are by far the best of all insect pollinators. They gather both pollen and nectar and store both for their young. They live in large communities, with thousands of worker bees to visit flowers. These workers (infertile females) fly cease-lessly back and forth until they literally work themselves to death.

Almost all flowers are honeybee-flowers. But there are a few exceptions. Some blossoms are too small for a worker's body to enter. Some are so tightly closed she cannot push them open. In some, the nectar is too deep for her tongue, which is only one fourth of an inch long. Some are the wrong color. A bee's eyes can recognize only the spectrum from yellow through blue to ultraviolet; so she often ignores red flowers, but is especially fond of blue ones.

The bee performs her tasks best when she can find the nectar in a flower quickly and easily. Then she can move on im-mediately and carry pollen to many other waiting stigmas.

In some flowers, generally rather primitive types like the but-tercup, there is nothing to guide the bee. The petals are spread in a horizontal circle. She can land on them anywhere, facing in any direction. She may waste valuable minutes looking for the pollen and nectar, even though they are usually in easy reach.

22

BUTTERCUP

But other plants have aids that show the bee exactly where to go. Their flowers provide landing platforms (usually enlarged petals), honey-guides, and other insect aids. All this, of course, influences the shapes of the flower parts. It results in forms which sometimes appear very strange until we learn how they fit a particular insect need.

A sage flower is a good example. It belongs to the highly evolved Mint family. And it has a most remarkable pollinating system—a far cry from that of the simple buttercup. Flowers of the blue-sage thrust forward a large petal which the bee lands on. Its bright spots are honey-guides that lead her into a tubular throat. There she can not avoid touching the two stamens,

BLUE-SAGE

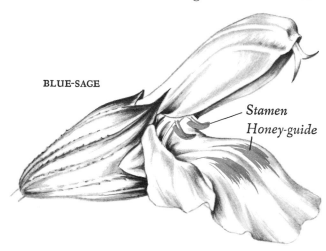

Stamen

Honey-guide

which grow from the wall of this throat. As the picture shows, the stamens are attached in such a way that the two ends of the filament are free to move up and down like a seesaw.

When a bee enters the mouth of the flower, her head pushes up the lower filament end. This causes the upper end, with its anther, to clamp suddenly down on her back. The anther leaves its dab of pollen, ready to be carried on the bee's body to another blossom.

During the time that the flower has pollen to shed, its pistil is held high against the uppermost petal. There the stigma is well out of the way of the pollen-loading operations below. But when the anthers have finished shedding their pollen, the pistil comes into action. It grows longer until it hangs down in the mouth of the flower. There each approaching bee will find it, in exactly the right place to catch the dab of pollen on her back.

This mechanism of the blue-sage will work for us as well as for the bee. All we have to do is gently push a pencil point into the throat of the flower. Immediately the seesaw stamens will snap down. In the same way, we can operate the similar, but even more dramatic, "stamen machine" of the clary-sage.

We can set off the startling trigger devices of many other flowers. Barberry stamens, for instance, move inward and touch the head of a visiting bee. The stamens of mountain-laurel spring out of tiny pockets in the corolla wall and throw their pollen against the insect. Flowers of the Pea family keep their stamens tightly wrapped in a pair of petals. The touch of an insect's tongue (or a pin point) at the base of the honey-guide releases them with a snap. There are hundreds of such mechanisms. They vary in relation to the bodies and habits of the insects they are intended to serve.

24

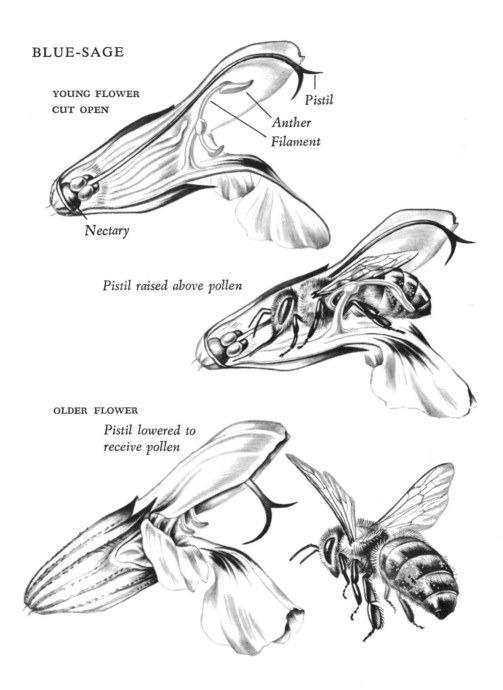

BLUE-SAGE

YOUNG FLOWER
CUT OPEN

Pistil

Anther

Filament

Nectary

Pistil raised above pollen

OLDER FLOWER

Pistil lowered to
receive pollen

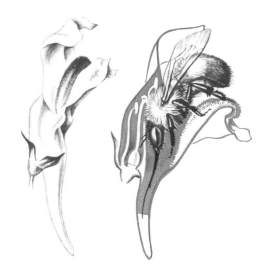

MONKSHOOD

TOADFLAX

Bumblebees are almost exactly the same as honeybees in their collecting habits. But they are bigger and stronger and have longer tongues (up to ten-sixteenths of an inch). They can force their way into the tightly closed blossoms of toadflax, turtlehead, and closed-gentian. They can set off the stiffest trigger flowers of the Pea family. They can reach into the long nectaries of nasturtium, larkspur, and jewelweed. Monkshood and red-clover, with their long nectaries, are exclusively bumble-bee-flowers. They grow only where there are bumblebees to pollinate them.

Butterflies and moths by no means rival bees as pollinators, but they are important to many flowers with deep nectaries. They eat only nectar, which they suck up through their very long tongues. These tongues quite commonly equal the insect's

BUTTERFLY-FLOWERS

FIRE-PINK

BUTTERFLY-WEED

body in length, but they vary greatly. One tropical moth has a proboscis eleven inches long.

Butterflies and moths differ from each other in a number of ways. But, so far as the flower is concerned, the most important difference is that one flies by day, the other by night. Butterflies are sun lovers. Butterfly-flowers bloom in the daytime and often close at night. Such blossoms are bright in color. Many are red, and butterflies seem to like this part of the spectrum.

The butterfly drinks most comfortably from a long, narrow tube, which suits his long tongue. And he always sits as he eats. He may come to rest on the large petal of a single blossom like fire-pink or phlox. Or he may perch on the surface formed by a cluster of small florets, like those of butterfly-weed or sunflower.

27

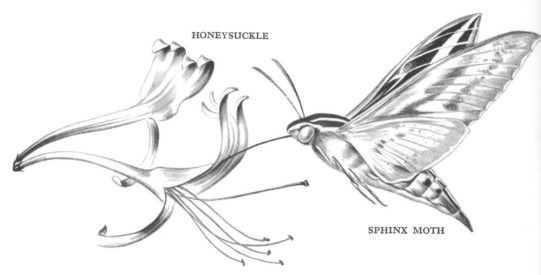

HONEYSUCKLE

SPHINX MOTH

Moth-flowers meet the somewhat different needs of night-flying insects. Moths dart through the garden like small hummingbirds. They drink as they hover in front of a flower, never coming to rest on it. Therefore landing platforms are not necessary. Petals are often curled back and out of the way. Most moths have a keen sense of smell and are guided to flowers chiefly by fragrance. But in addition, for maximum visibility, night-blooming flowers are usually white. (Though the great majority of moths are nocturnal, there are some day-flying species, with habits like those of butterflies.)

In the tropics, hummingbirds are important pollinizers. They drink on the wing as moths do. But they fly by day and are especially fond of red flowers.

A great many kinds of flies pollinate flowers. Some eat pollen or nectar and visit flowers much as bees do. They often look so much like bees that it is hard to tell the difference. (Flies always have two wings; bees have four.)

But other flies are so unskilled that they do their pollinating only when a plant seems to trick them into it. Many of them

28

feed on decaying flesh or vegetation. The strong odor of these materials is as attractive to them as it is unattractive to us. Fly-flowers often imitate it and so attract the unsuspecting insects. Carrion-flower and skunk-cabbage, for example, are fertilized by flies which visit them because of their smell and not for either pollen or nectar. Some fly-flowers even imitate the look of decaying matter: trillium, with its brownish-purple color; jack-in-the-pulpit, with its streaked canopy; some saxifrages, with their speckled petals.

Some plants—like jack-in-the-pulpit and its European cousin, cuckoo-pint—actually trap the flies. The insects are kept in the narrow tubes of the sheath while both pistils and stamens ripen. Only when pollination is complete are they allowed to fly away. Sometimes they die before they have a chance to escape.

FLY-FLOWERS

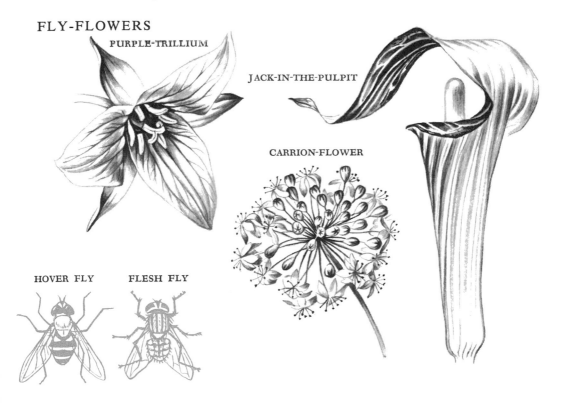

PURPLE-TRILLIUM

JACK-IN-THE-PULPIT

CARRION-FLOWER

HOVER FLY

FLESH FLY

BEETLE

ANT

All these insects are important pollinizers. Most others are unwelcome guests, who may visit flowers for food but who carry no pollen in return.

Beetles are on the borderline. There are species which pollinate flowers, but they usually do it because they like to eat the flower itself. They cause so much damage that only a few plants find them useful as pollinators. Beetles have wings, but they do not fly rapidly from blossom to blossom. And their smooth, hard bodies do not easily pick up and hold pollen. Beetle-flowers are mostly primitive, like the magnolia.

Ants are typical robber insects. Their smooth bodies carry no pollen. They have no wings and are limited in their travels. They are of no assistance to the flower, and every precaution is taken to shut them out.

Certain plant structures discourage robbers. Some stems are hard for crawling insects to climb because they are extremely slippery or else covered with sticky hairs. Sometimes the throats of flowers are blocked by thick "fur" or a fringe of bristles. Most of the time, however, the relation between flowers and insects is a friendly one. Each provides the other with the basic essentials of survival.

Other Kinds of Pollination

Many botanists think that wind pollination is the oldest and most primitive method of pollen distribution and that it was the only method for millions of years. Its efficiency is proved by the great numbers of plants which still use it.

Though some of these are primitive, many are highly specialized. They include nearly all our trees and grasses, and

30

many other plants as well. Most of them bloom very early in the spring, before thick foliage can break the flight of pollen through the air.

These flowers have no need to advertise, since wind will come to them whether invited or not. They require neither landing platforms nor honey-guides, so the corolla is relieved of all its ordinary duties. It might even be a handicap if it cut off the air currents which carry pollen. Therefore, wind-flowers never have large, bright corollas. Petals are either missing entirely or they are small and dull in color. Generally they are green or greenish-yellow.

The calyx is usually small too. But it is often very tough, to protect these early flowers from cold.

Stamens and pistils, however, must be prominent. Long filaments dangle the anthers in the breeze. And all pistils have very furry or feathery stigmas to catch the pollen as it floats by.

Doing without corollas saves a great deal of material and energy. This is fortunate, since a tremendous amount of material must go into manufacturing great clouds of pollen. There must be enough pollen so that some of it is sure to fall on the

TYPICAL WIND-FLOWER

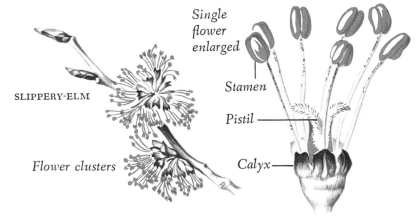

SLIPPERY-ELM

Flower clusters

Single flower enlarged

Stamen

Pistil

Calyx

right pistils. And each grain must have an extra-hard coat to keep it from drying out. Even so, wind-carried pollen lasts only a few hours.

The anthers open on sunny, breezy days. Too much wind wastes pollen by carrying it off too rapidly in one direction. Too little wind allows it to drop without traveling to another plant. On the right kind of day, we can stir up our own yellow clouds by jiggling a handful of grasses or breathing on the hanging catkins of birch or oak or walnut.

Wind-flowers seldom attract our eyes. The ones which grow on trees, for instance, are so small and so inconspicuous that

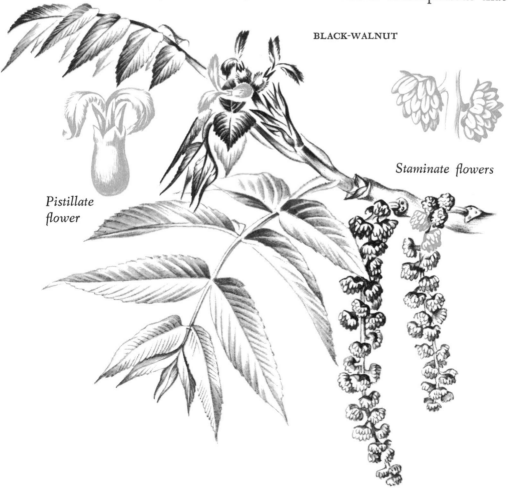

BLACK-WALNUT

Staminate flowers

Pistillate flower

many people think trees have no flowers at all. But the tiny blossoms are surprisingly beautiful when we look at them closely. We can still recognize the usual flower parts, though they may seem peculiar in shape. Some have been changed to meet the requirements of a special way of life. Others have disappeared because they were no longer needed.

Staminate flowers

In wind-flowers we can find examples of all the familiar devices for cross pollination. Very commonly, especially among trees, the pistils and stamens grow in separate flowers. The staminate flowers often hang in long, flexible catkins. They move easily in the wind to scatter their pollen. Pistillate flowers are more likely to be held rigidly on the tip of a twig. They stand comparatively still, waiting for pollen to fall on them. When both types grow on a single branch, the pistillate flowers are usually carried well above the pollen-bearing ones.

Ragweed is an exception to this, with its pistillate flowers at the bottom of its long flower spike. But otherwise its tiny green blossoms are typical wind-flowers. And in late summer it fills the air with the pollen that brings so much human misery. (Hay fever is caused almost entirely by wind-pollinated plants. Insect pollen is sticky and heavy and does not fly about. It can irritate a sensitive nose only when that nose actually touches the stamens of an insect-flower.)

RAGWEED

Pistillate flowers

Thus, with the help of wind or insects, plants receive the foreign pollen which most of them need. But there are plants which seem not to need it and which regularly fertilize themselves. Their self pollination is a normal and reliable method of seed-making. It is quite a different matter from the last-minute emergency measures other flowers sometimes use.

We find self fertilization often in the Pea family. Here, pistils and stamens are enclosed so tightly that insects have a hard time reaching them. Some of these flowers are triggered by the right kind of bee, but many are self pollinated.

Certain grasses always pollinate themselves. The anthers and stigmas mature while still inside the bud. By the time the bud opens, the job is done.

However, the most interesting device for self pollination occurs in such plants as meadow-violet, fringed-polygala, and hog-peanut. Though they all have fairly showy blossoms, with good arrangements for insect pollination, they also have a second set of buds of a special kind.

In the meadow-violet, these buds appear just as the bright spring bloom is ending and then continue in a long succession

Closed flower

MEADOW-VIOLET

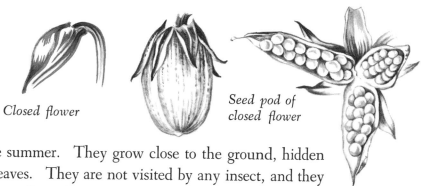

Closed flower

Seed pod of closed flower

through the summer. They grow close to the ground, hidden under the leaves. They are not visited by any insect, and they never open at all. The anthers and stigmas lie close together inside the bud, and the pollen tubes grow through the anther walls into the stigmas. After this hidden fertilization, the ovaries grow into pods literally bursting with seeds.

These *cleistogamous* flowers get their name from two Greek words meaning "closed marriage." They are found in nearly all species of violets. They may vary in shape and may grow at the top of the stem as well as under the leaves, but they are all alike in producing great quantities of seeds.

It seems strange that such a good insect-plant would have to use this second method of insuring fruits. But the violet blooms very early, when there are not many insects about. A cold and stormy spring might keep away most of its usual pollinators. Or its anthers or stigmas might be frozen. The tiny closed flowers are a safeguard, to provide seeds in spite of all mishaps.

And they do this supremely well. Though the violet's bright insect-flowers take care of cross breeding, the cleistogamous buds are the ones which manufacture thousands of seeds at little cost to the plant. In late summer, when they are ripe, they snap open and shoot seeds far and wide. So it is these little blind flowers, working in secret, which are most responsible for the carpets of violets spread each year over every field and woodland.

35

Flower Parts

The development of these closed flowers gives us an idea of the causes and ways of plant evolution. Changing conditions mean changing plant habits. A very dry season, for instance, will often cause flowers to rush their seed-making. They may bloom earlier than normal or ripen their seeds before reaching their usual size. If such a weather condition occurred often or became permanent, the plants' reaction might become permanent too. The early-blooming members of the species would be the ones which survived. And this habit would in time become a built-in characteristic of the race.

Thus plants "adapt themselves." But it is important to remember that this is not done by any conscious effort or by any single plant. Factors called *genes* inside the plant cells are responsible for its heredity. Various combinations of these genes produce the various outer forms of leaf or flower. Any form which gives a plant an advantage over its fellows will likely keep

36

it alive and fruiting. And its less fortunate neighbors may well be crowded out before they can produce seed.

If this happens over and over, a great number of plants, in a long series of generations, can accomplish what could never be done by one plant in one generation. This kind of change has been going on for millions of years. Plants and insects have developed together and influenced each other. And so we have all the myriad shapes and colors of today's floral world.

Such change and experiment may occur in any part of the plant. In the flower, the changes are all for the purpose of producing the best possible seeds with the least possible material. When flowers first began to evolve, they were lavishly wasteful. They were all wind pollinated and had to manufacture unbelievable quantities of pollen. Even after insects began to carry the pollen, each flower had many pistils, many stamens, many petals. In spite of the waste, some of those flowers survived. And they still flourish, with all their primitive characteristics.

Among them are the magnolia, the mousetail, the buttercup. They all have the simplest possible arrangement of their floral parts. Their petals are all alike and grow in a ring. Inside this, the stamens appear in another ring. And inside this, in turn, is the cluster of pistils.

Each flower bears enough ovules to produce dozens of seeds. But only a few of those ovules will ever reach the point of becoming new plants. In the first place, very few will be fertilized. These primitive flowers do nothing to guide the insect visitor. He can land anywhere and move in any direction. Sometimes he touches the pistil and stamens; sometimes he does not.

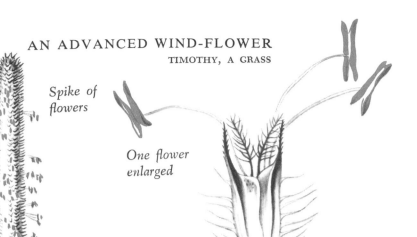

AN ADVANCED WIND-FLOWER
TIMOTHY, A GRASS

Spike of flowers

One flower enlarged

Still more waste occurs through loss of pollen and nectar. Since they are unprotected, they can easily be stolen by robber insects or damaged by rain or heat. Therefore, extra large quantities must be manufactured.

Very, very gradually, more efficient flowers developed. Their present-day descendants usually have fewer parts. Many of them produce fewer seeds and so are able to give each seed more food and care. Among wind-pollinated plants, the most highly developed ones are the grasses. Of insect-plants, the most advanced ones include orchids, mints, and members of the Composite family.

Mint flowers, for instance, are in every way different from buttercups and magnolias. Their few petals are joined into a tubular corolla. This gives the insect just one place to land and one path to follow to the nectar. Mints never have more than four stamens and one pistil. And these are placed so that a visitor cannot help touching the pollen. Pollen and nectar are so well shielded that very little is lost by accident. And each flower contents itself with four well-nourished seeds.

38

The road between these lowest and highest forms was long. The number of variations which appeared and vanished again is beyond imagination. Many steps in the process led nowhere. But many others led to new plants that proved to be successful and so lived on. By studying the forms of today's flowers—like the magnolia and the mint—we can trace some of this slow and intricate development.

A few general rules govern the process: Its aim, as we know, is to produce the best offspring with the least expense of energy and material. Flower parts which are used get first chance at the available material. Thus, if great numbers of pistils become useless, they gradually disappear. If one part is increased in size, another part will be decreased. If one petal is enlarged into a landing-platform, other petals will become smaller. Material saved in one part is available for use in another.

Since insects and plants are so closely bound up with each other, we know that the two must have traveled this long evolutionary road together. There is no way of telling whether a

AN ADVANCED INSECT-FLOWER

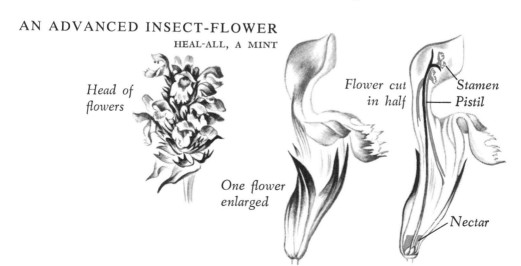

HEAL-ALL, A MINT

Head of flowers

One flower enlarged

Flower cut in half

Stamen

Pistil

Nectar

certain flower changed to fit a certain insect, or the insect to fit the flower. But it could have happened either way.

We do know, however, that the form of any flower is governed by the needs of its pollinizing agent. For instance, the shapes of parts in two of our common wild lilies are easily understood as soon as we are acquainted with their insect pollinizers. The Canada-lily and the red wood-lily are very much alike in size and color and geographical range. But the Canada-lily is pollinated by bees and the wood-lily by butterflies, and this accounts for all their differences.

The bee-lily hangs downward like a bell. Insects which visit it cling to the pistil and stamens as they crawl up into its cup. The flower of the butterfly-lily, on the other hand, stands erect, and its insect visitors perch on the outturned petals. Its cup would soon fill with water if it were shaped like the Canada-lily. But the lower part of each petal is narrowed into a *claw*. This leaves wide openings between the petals through which the rain can escape.

Even more important is the groove formed by the inrolled edges of each claw. This groove just fits a butterfly's tongue and guides it down to the nectar gland at the base of the petal. As the insect reaches into the flower, his wings brush the pistil and stamens.

A cousin of these two—the white Bermuda or Easter-lily— differs from them in color, position, and fragrance, all because it caters to the needs of night-flying moths.

So pollination is the end and the beginning. It carries the key to nearly all the floral mysteries which surround us everywhere, waiting to be discovered by any clear eye and understanding mind.

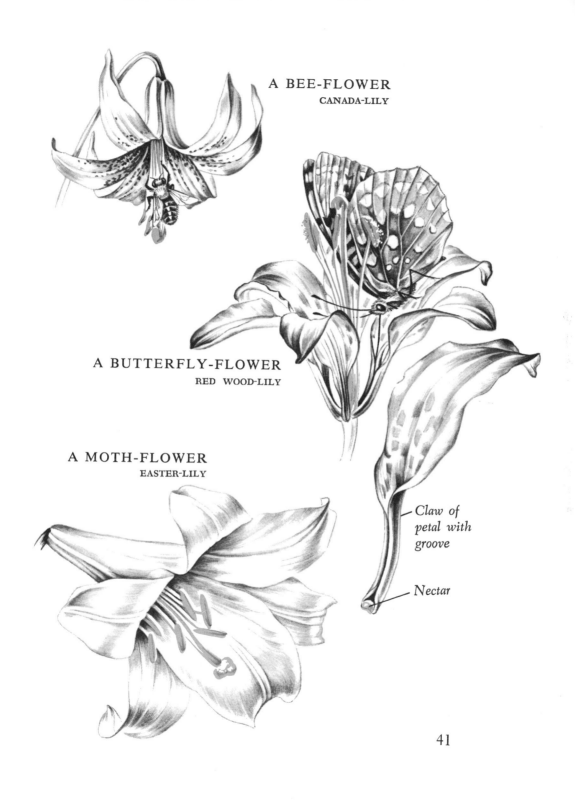

A BEE-FLOWER
CANADA-LILY

A BUTTERFLY-FLOWER
RED WOOD-LILY

A MOTH-FLOWER
EASTER-LILY

*Claw of
petal with
groove*

Nectar

41

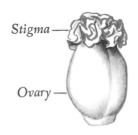

Stigma —

Ovary —

Pistils

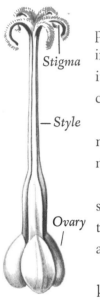

Stigma

— Style

Ovary

Every part of a flower has some large or small share in the process of seed-making, but stamens and pistils play the most important roles. The pistil, or female organ, is essential, since it must bear the seeds. Each of its parts is designed so that it can do this with the greatest efficiency.

The pistil of the wild geranium (page 9) is a fairly common type. We might examine it again, now that we know more about the meaning of flower parts.

The ovary at the base of the pistil holds the tiny ovules or seeds-to-be, protecting and nourishing them. After fertilization, the ovules grow into seeds. The ovary grows with them and becomes what is commonly called a seed pod.

The stigma at the top of the geranium pistil is at first a mere knob. When mature, it spreads open its five arms, each with a fuzzy receptive surface to catch pollen. The work of the stigma is over when the ovules are fertilized. Then, in most flowers, it shrivels and drops off. But sometimes, as in the geranium, it remains attached to the top of the seed pod.

The geranium stigma, in order to touch the insect at the right place, must be raised some distance above the ovary. Therefore it needs a stalk, or style. A style, unlike an ovary and a stigma, is not always necessary. In some flowers, like the may-apple, the pistil has no style. Then the stigma rests directly on top of the ovary.

42

PRIMITIVE PISTIL

BUTTERCUP

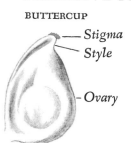

— Stigma
— Style

– Ovary

WIND-FLOWER PISTILS

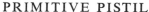

POPLAR

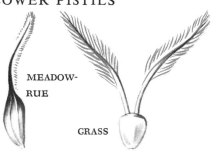

MEADOW-RUE

GRASS

The first flowers had pistils like those still found in buttercup and magnolia. Each was primitive in shape and contained one ovule. From these beginnings evolved hundreds of variations, all designed to fit certain specific pollinizing agents.

Wind-flower pistils are still comparatively simple and do not vary much. Their one important requirement is a very furry stigma, spread out to catch the pollen grains in the air. They seldom need long styles. Since wind-flowers usually have no petals, the whole pistil is uncovered. Therefore the stigma does not need to be lifted up on a stalk.

The pistils of insect-flowers have evolved into every imaginable shape. The ovary may be a ball or a tube or an irregular pouch. Styles may be long or short, fat or thin, one or several. Stigmas range in shape from the tiny button tips of toothwort and rhododendron to the elaborate petal-like forms of iris and pitcher-plant. They may be either smooth or fuzzy. But they must always have some kind of sticky surface to receive and hold the pollen.

INSECT-FLOWER PISTILS

TOOTHWORT

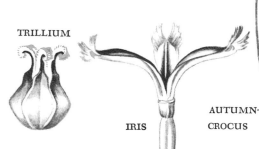

TRILLIUM

IRIS

AUTUMN-CROCUS

NUMEROUS SIMPLE PISTILS

WOOD-ANEMONE

One pistil cut open

Group of pistils

Ovule

In the beginning, pistils were not only very simple, but also very numerous. Sometimes there were as many as a hundred in a single flower. We still find a good many of these "old-fashioned" blossoms. Arrowhead, marsh-marigold, and anemone, for instance, all bear a large group of separate, simple pistils.

But the processes of evolution have changed the number of pistils as well as their shape. Some flowers, like the apricot and all the Pea family, now do very well with only one. Other

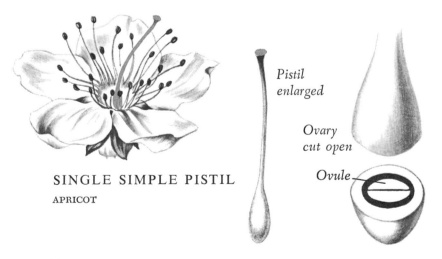

SINGLE SIMPLE PISTIL

APRICOT

Pistil enlarged

Ovary cut open

Ovule

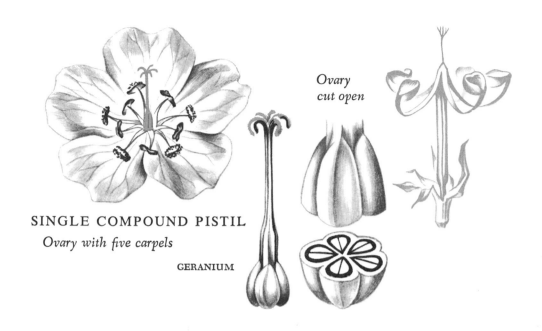

SINGLE COMPOUND PISTIL

Ovary with five carpels

GERANIUM

Ovary cut open

flowers still have several of the original number—three or four or five, perhaps. But often this whole group is united into a single body and looks like a single pistil.

This is true in the geranium. If we cut through its ovary with a sharp knife, we can see what happened. The ovary is made up of five compartments like the segments of an orange. Each of these segments is called a *carpel*. And each carpel is really a pistil—or rather the descendant of an ancient pistil—joined to its neighbors. In a sense, the geranium still has five pistils, joined together throughout most of their length. Only the five stigmas are still separate. They form the five pollen-catching arms. And the five ovaries reappear as separate cups when the seed pod splits open.

A union of carpels like this is called a *compound pistil*. Such a pistil may have any number of carpels from two to fifteen or

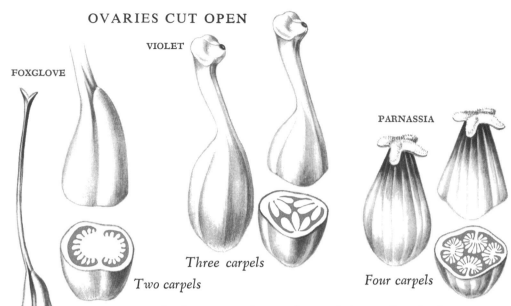

OVARIES CUT OPEN

FOXGLOVE

VIOLET

PARNASSIA

Two carpels

Three carpels

Four carpels

more. Inside the ovary, the ovules and the walls which separate them may be arranged in various ways. And sometimes the walls have disappeared. But usually the divisions show up clearly, and we can easily see how many carpels there are.

Even without cutting the ovary open, we can count carpels by counting the number of stigma arms or the sections of a ripe seed pod. Sometimes the carpels are visible as bulges or ridges on the outside of the ovary.

This union of pistils is a practical arrangement. It saves material and increases the likelihood of pollination. An insect can easily scatter pollen on all five branches of a stigma in one visit, whereas he might have to make five visits to pollinate five separate stigmas.

So the compound pistil has been successful and is the commonest type today. The number of its carpels usually—though not always—matches the general number plan of the whole flower.

46

These number plans are very important for the study of plant relationships. In lilies and their relatives, for instance, the flower parts—carpels, stamens, petals, sepals—are typically arranged in groups of three. In other plants, the number plans may be based on four or five.

Every pistil—simple or compound, solitary or part of a group —will mature if even one of its ovules is fertilized. The ovules ripen into seeds and the ovary becomes a *fruit*. This is the correct name for any ripe seed container. It does not have to be at all like the fruits we buy in the market.

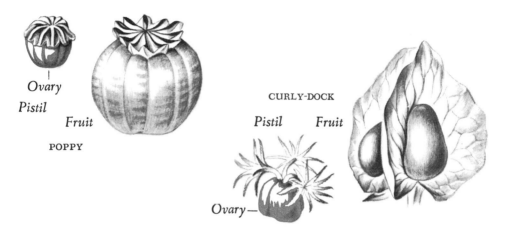

Ovary

Pistil

Fruit

POPPY

CURLY-DOCK

Pistil   Fruit

Ovary—

The fruit sometimes looks much like the ovary, but often it has changed considerably during growth. It may be either hard and dry or soft and fleshy—a berry, a nut, a capsule, a grain, a pod. Finally it either splits open or slowly disintegrates. Then the seeds are set free and are ready to be scattered about. Sometimes they fly on wings of their own. Sometimes they must be transported, by birds or animals or man, to their new and often distant homes.

47

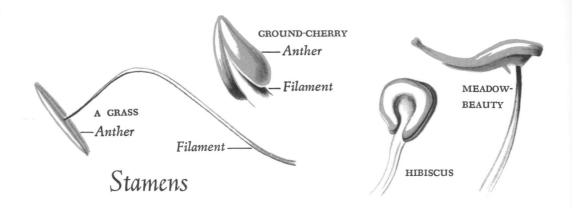

GROUND-CHERRY
—*Anther*

—*Filament*

A GRASS
—*Anther*

Filament —

MEADOW-
BEAUTY

HIBISCUS

Stamens

Stamens are the male organs of a flower. Their pollen carries the sperm cells which can stir to life the minute egg cells waiting within an ovule.

As we know, a stamen has two parts: The anther manufactures and stores pollen. The filament holds the anther in the position best suited for the removal of pollen. In flowers where filaments are not needed, they have—like the useless styles—partly or wholly disappeared. But anthers, of course, are always essential.

Among present-day blossoms, stamens differ in size and shape as much as pistils do. Their filaments may be the long delicate threads of a wind-pollinated grass. Or they may be short, stubby blades like those of the ground-cherry. Some filaments are feathered, some are furry, some are ridged. Some even bear the nectaries. Anthers also vary in shape and in the way they are attached to the filaments.

Stamens have evolved just as all other flower parts have. The trend of evolution, of course, is toward saving material and energy, and at the same time producing the best possible seeds. Therefore, numerous parts have often evolved to a few; separate parts have been united; some parts have been changed in position to improve the chances of pollination.

48

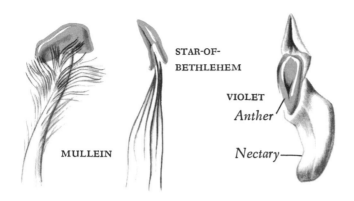

STAR-OF-BETHLEHEM

VIOLET

Anther

Nectary

MULLEIN

In primitive flowers, stamens were as numerous as pistils. There are still some blossoms, like magnolia and waterlily, which bear them in dozens or even in hundreds. Such a large mass of stamens is sometimes an advantage. They can help attract insects and they produce a great deal of pollen.

But a much smaller number of stamens does the same thing more economically and almost as well. So now most plants have only a few. In such cases, the stamens are arranged in one or two simple rings like those of the geranium. And they conform to the number plan of the flower, with one or two stamens to match each petal.

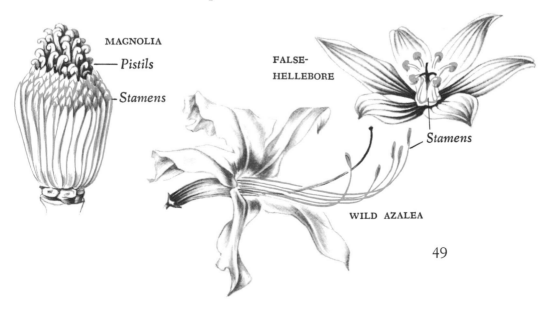

MAGNOLIA

— *Pistils*

— *Stamens*

FALSE-HELLEBORE

Stamens

WILD AZALEA

49

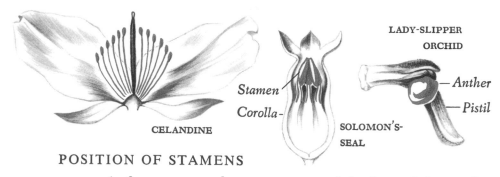

Stamen
Corolla-

CELANDINE

SOLOMON'S-
SEAL

LADY-SLIPPER
ORCHID

—Anther
—Pistil

POSITION OF STAMENS

At first, stamens always grew around the base of the pistils, and this is still where they most commonly occur. But in some flowers they have been raised onto the corolla wall. Such an arrangement is a great advantage in tubular blossoms, where very long filaments would be necessary to hold the anthers high enough. Much material is saved when the filaments are shortened and attached high on the inside wall of the flower. In the Orchid family, this saving is accomplished by joining the anthers to the sides of the pistil.

Stamens are not united as often as pistils are. They generally distribute pollen better if they are not too close together. But sometimes either the filaments or the anthers are joined.

In the common Saint-John's-wort and all the various citrus flowers, the filaments are fastened together in bundles of five or so. In the Pea family and the mallows, the united filaments form a tube around the pistil. These arrangements save material, but they do not greatly affect the methods of pollination.

UNITED FILAMENTS

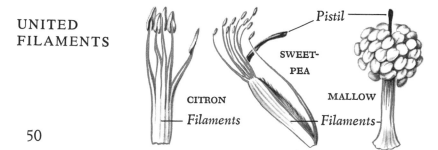

Pistil —

SWEET-
PEA

CITRON

— Filaments

MALLOW

Filaments—

50

United anthers, however, result in some very unusual pollinating devices. They occur only in highly specialized flowers
like the lobelias and the composites. A good example is found
in the small center florets of the sunflower.

The joined anthers form a tube around the pistil and shed
their pollen inside the tube. Upward through this tube grows
the pistil. The stigma is tightly closed to keep its sensitive surface from touching the pollen. Its outer surfaces are covered
with a stiff brush of hairs.

As it grows, the brush pushes the pollen mass up and finally
out the end of the anther tube. Here the pollen is held for a
while, to be carried off by insects. Then the stigma at last
opens into two receptive arms.

UNITED ANTHERS, SUNFLOWER

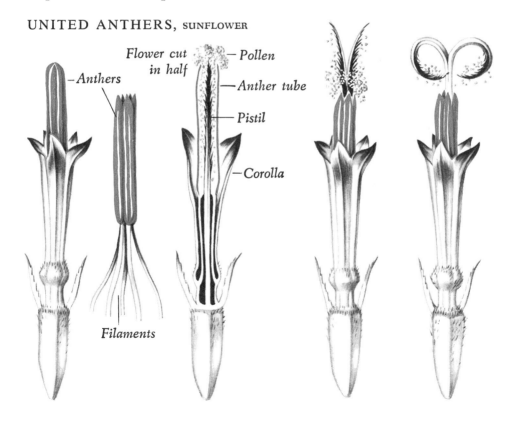

Flower cut in half — Pollen
—Anthers
—Anther tube
—Pistil
—Corolla
Filaments

Some flowers have puzzling structures growing where we would expect to find stamens. In parnassia, for instance, we easily recognize the five normal-looking stamens. They have large, fat anthers and they alternate with the five white petals. But in between them are bundles of what appear to be a different kind of stamen. These are very tiny, with bright yellow tips. They are *staminodes*, or stamens which produce no pollen. In parnassia they serve as honey-guides.

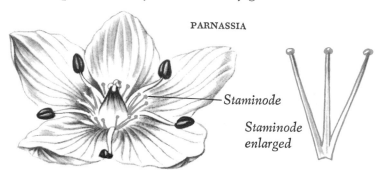

PARNASSIA

Staminode

Staminode
enlarged

Staminodes occur in may flowers. They have a variety of forms and they serve many purposes. Sometimes they help attract insects. Sometimes they secrete nectar. Sometimes they protect the pistils. Sometimes they seem to be useless leftovers from the days when primitive flowers had many stamens.

Since the anther is the most important part of a stamen, we might well examine it more closely. It is sometimes called a little bag to hold pollen, but it is not quite so simple as that. A typical anther is really two little bags, or *lobes*. The lobes are separated by a strip of tissue—usually the end of the filament. Each lobe is originally formed of two tiny sacs. But these sacs usually fuse into one by the time the anther is mature.

When it is ripe, the anther opens and sheds its pollen. Most commonly, each lobe splits from end to end. The edges of the

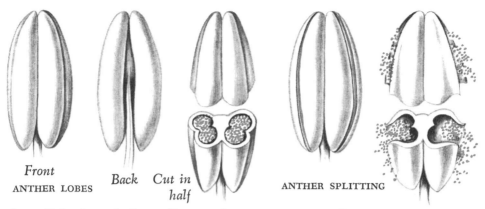

Front
ANTHER LOBES

Back *Cut in half*

ANTHER SPLITTING

slit roll back and the pollen pushes out in a powdery mass.

But this is not the only method of releasing pollen. Some anthers open with "trap doors" like those of barberry and sassafras. Some, like woody-nightshade and mountain-laurel, have a small round hole or pore in the end of each lobe. In other members of the Heath family, this hole is at the end of a little tube or horn.

Anthers often contrast with the color of the petals. Thus they help to serve as honey-guides. Those of the white bearberry are red. Those of purple-loosestrife are emerald green. Those of the pinky-white marshmallow are lavender. But yellow and yellow-green are the most common. Of course, once the anther is opened, its true color is often hidden by the mass of pollen, which is usually yellow.

TYPES OF ANTHERS

SASSAFRAS   MOUNTAIN-LAUREL   BEARBERRY

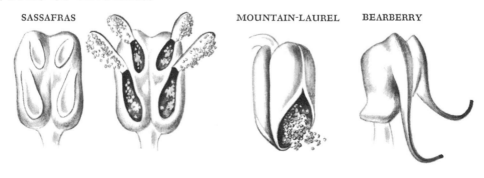

Individual pollen grains, or spores, are so small they can be seen only through a microscope. But this "dust of the flower" bursts out of the anthers in enormous quantities. It seems wasteful when we remember that just one grain is enough to fertilize an ovule. But thousands of grains serve as payment to insects. Other thousands will be lost without finding a receptive stigma. Many are damaged by rain or dried up by heat.

In order to cut down this kind of loss, each tiny spore is covered with a protective coat. If the pollen is to be carried long distances by the wind, the coat is generally very hard and smooth. And the grain is more or less spherical in form. The pollen of insect-flowers, on the other hand, is likely to have spines or ridges or a sticky coating to catch on the bodies of insects. These grains can vary widely in shape.

Sometimes pollen grains are bound loosely together with delicate threads, as in the mountain-laurel. Sometimes they are united in fours, as in other members of the Heath family. And sometimes the pollen is not powdery at all. It clings together in waxy or sticky masses called *pollinia*. These we find in the highly specialized flowers of orchids and milkweeds.

Pollen grains are often beautiful, and they are always important. They carry from one flower to another the gifts of life and of new heredity for its offspring.

The Corolla

The corolla—the "little crown" of petals—usually seems the most dramatic part of a flower. Of course, it has no direct share in the seed-making. But in insect-flowers at least, it is almost as necessary as the pistils and stamens themselves. If the

54

corolla were not there, those vital organs would seldom succeed in carrying out their functions.

Nearly always pistils and stamens stick closely to their basic work and do nothing else. But the responsibilities of the corolla are many and varied. First of all, it must attract the attention of insects. In the world of plants, there is fierce competition for the services of the various pollinizers, and advertising is as important as it is in present-day America. Thus the petals are a kind of insect billboard, announcing the presence of pollen or nectar.

Then, after the guests are invited, the corolla must provide for their needs. It offers them a place to land, a cupful of nectar, and a guide to that honey-store.

In addition, it must often protect the honey-store. Nectar and pollen and sensitive stigmas are easily damaged by cold and rain. If they are not shielded—by corolla or calyx or both —there will be almost certain loss. And replacing such a loss may be an expensive business for the flower.

The part the corolla plays in all this decides whether it will be large and showy or completely lacking. In most wind-flowers, as we know, petals are missing because they would only be in the way of flying pollen. Occasionally they are missing in insect-flowers too. But then the sepals nearly always replace them, taking on both the look and the duties of a corolla.

No corolla
LIZARD'S-TAIL

Like other flower parts, petals were originally separate and very numerous. And they always grew in a simple ring or spiral at the base of the stamens. Now they are fewer—often three or four or five. But these few are likely to have much more variety of size and shape and position. It is to these

55

corolla variations, more than to anything else, that flowers owe their particular characters—their "personalities."

Petals, however, are not always varied. In some cases, they all do the same work in the same way. Then they remain alike in shape and position. This results in simple flowers with separate petals, like the geranium and wild rose. Such blossoms are saucer-shaped or wheel-shaped, with petals all radiating out from the center. Because of this uniform arrangement, they are called *regular flowers*.

Flowers with separate petals are more primitive than those with united petals. But even so they have evolved into a great variety of forms.

Sometimes, as in the Carnation and Mustard families, they appear to have united corollas. The regular petals of the saucer spread out at the top of a tube, as though their lower ends were joined. But, if we pull a flower apart, we will find the petals all quite separate. They are merely elongated into narrow claws. And the claws are held close together inside the calyx.

REGULAR FLOWERS WITH SEPARATE PETALS

Many petals
BITTERROOT

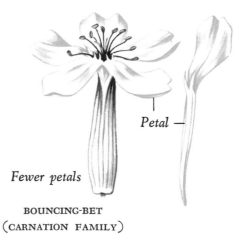

Petal —

Fewer petals

BOUNCING-BET
(CARNATION FAMILY)

IRREGULAR FLOWERS
WITH SEPARATE PETALS

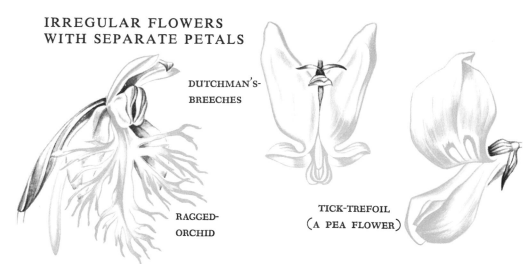

DUTCHMAN'S-
BREECHES

RAGGED-
ORCHID

TICK-TREFOIL
(A PEA FLOWER)

Sometimes the separate-petaled flowers are *irregular*. The saucer shape is lost because one or more petals have been changed. They now perform some special job of guidance or protection or nectar storage which the old, flat petals could not do.

The irregularity may be very slight, as in horsechestnut flowers; or very pronounced, as in columbine and dutchman's-breeches. In these two, the unusual shape is due to the long nectaries. In the ragged-orchid, one big fringed petal is extended as a landing platform. In a Pea flower, one petal serves as a banner, two form a landing platform, and two more tightly sheath the stamens and pistil. The polygala has a somewhat similar arrangement, tipped with a fringe to attract insects.

However, united petals can perform almost every one of these duties better than separate petals can. So it is not surprising that this is the arrangement which most often provides drinking tubes for butterflies or tunnels for bees. United petals save material. They also give by far the best protection to pollen and nectar and the best guidance to insects.

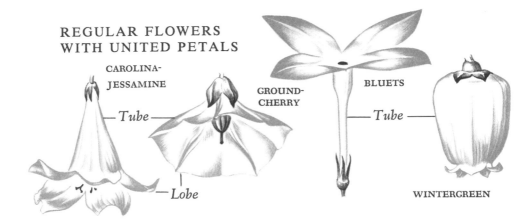

REGULAR FLOWERS
WITH UNITED PETALS

CAROLINA-
JESSAMINE

GROUND-
CHERRY

BLUETS

Tube

Tube

Lobe

WINTERGREEN

The joined petals form a *tube*. It may be long or short; narrow or wide; shaped like a bell, a funnel, an urn, a bowl, or a cylinder. The outer tips of the petals are usually still separate and visible at the end of the tube. They are called *lobes*. They may be quite distinct, as in phlox and Carolina-jessamine; or very indistinct, as in morning-glory and ground-cherry.

United corollas, like divided ones, may be either regular or irregular. When they are regular, the petal lobes radiate out in the usual wheel-shaped pattern. When they are irregular, the resulting shapes may be wonderfully varied and even fantastic.

Such corollas flaunt the greatest variety of attractive banners. Their devices for landing and guidance are the most elaborate, their sheltering tubes and canopies the most effective. They have reached the peak of specialized design.

The corolla, naturally enough, is the place where we most often find striking and peculiar growths. Such are the trumpet of the daffodil, the corona of the milkweed, the slipper of the lady-slipper orchid. All these structures attract insects and serve as pollination mechanisms.

58

IRREGULAR FLOWERS WITH UNITED PETALS

CATALPA

— *Tube*

— *Lobe*

MOTHERWORT

FOXGLOVE

The "doubling" of petals may also attract insects. Though the main trend of evolution is from many parts to few, the process occasionally starts moving in the other direction. Once in a while, a plant will produce a variation, or *sport*, with more than the normal number of petals. Gardeners have eagerly seized upon them. Seed catalogues are full of double varieties of almost every species of garden flower.

But it would be interesting to know how many of these varieties could have survived the competition of nature. The extra petals might prove an advantage, since they would increase the visibility of the flower. But they might also use up more material and nourishment than the flower could afford to expend.

Petals, like any other flower part, can change in position as well as in number or shape. When the corolla changes position, it has a very important effect on the whole blossom.

By now, we are familiar with the basic positions of parts. We always expect to find the pistil in the center. It grows out of a platform called the *receptacle,* which is really just the enlarged end of the stem. Around and slightly below the pistil is the ring of stamens. Around and below the stamens are the petals. And around and below the petals are the sepals.

59

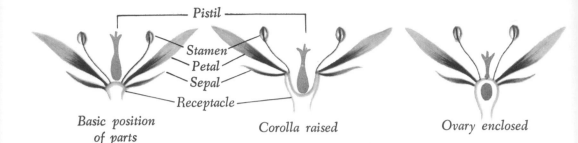

Pistil

Stamen
Petal
Sepal
Receptacle

Basic position of parts

Corolla raised

Ovary enclosed

To attract insects better, some flowers have evolved into a different arrangement. The corolla is raised. To accomplish this, the outer edges of the receptacle grew upward until they formed a cup around the ovary. The petals were carried up and left growing on the rim of the cup. And along with the petals went the stamens and sepals—incidentally improving their position too.

In many plants, the process did not stop there. The receptacle continued to grow over and around the ovary and completely enclosed it. This left the stamens, petals, and sepals all growing from the top of the ovary. The arrangement gives a distinctive shape to a flower, since the ovary looks like a base for the other parts. Because it is below those parts, it is called an *inferior ovary*. (A *superior ovary* is one in the original position, with the other parts around its base.)

In some flowers, the corolla was raised a second time. The evening-primrose has an inferior ovary. And above it is the cup—or narrow tube in this case—with stamens, petals, and sepals growing on its rim.

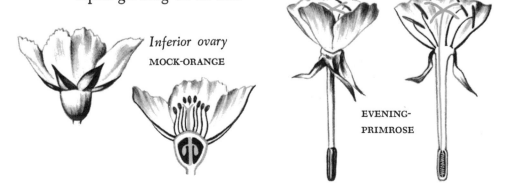

Inferior ovary
MOCK-ORANGE

EVENING-
PRIMROSE

GERANIUM

The Calyx

The calyx plays a small part in the drama of pollination. But it encloses and protects the other organs while they perform their vital duties. Without it, most blossoms could not live to maturity.

The calyx of our geranium is typical in structure and behavior. It has five separate sepals—one for each petal. They are green in color and heavier in texture than the petals. They enclose the bud until it opens. Later, after the petals drop, they envelop the growing seed pod. When the pod is ripe, the dried and shriveled sepals are still hanging below it.

Sepals may vary just as other flower parts do. They range from none at all—as in certain wind-flowers—to a great many—as in bitterroot. Most commonly, they match the petals in number. Their differences of shape and color seem endless. Sometimes their forms are so peculiar that the calyx can be recognized only by an expert.

These variations, of course, depend on the duties the calyx has to perform. First of all, it must protect the flower. It must be of a shape to enclose the bud, and it must be tough enough to withstand the weather. Sometimes—in flowers of early spring, like wild ginger—it even provides a fur coat.

The calyx is usually green. This indicates that it contains chlorophyl and can join the leaves in manufacturing sugar and starch. Sometimes it is tipped or streaked with other colors.

61

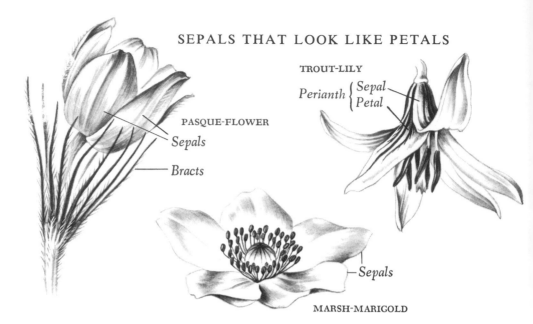

TROUT-LILY

Perianth { Sepal
{ Petal

PASQUE-FLOWER

Sepals

Bracts

Sepals

MARSH-MARIGOLD

Sometimes the green has disappeared entirely. Then the sepals are bright hued and they look like, and even function as, petals.

In lilies and similar flowers, the three sepals look almost exactly like the three petals. The six together are called the *perianth.* (Actually, "perianth" is the correct term for the combined calyx and corolla of any flower. But it is little used except in cases where petals and sepals are alike.)

Sometimes the sepals not only look like petals but completely replace them, as in marsh-marigold and Christmas-rose. And often, when the sepals replace the petals, other leafy parts replace the sepals. These leafy *bracts* (page 64) take over all the duties of a calyx, as in hepatica and pasque-flower.

Often the sepals have unusual or irregular shapes. Those of the wild rose are deeply cut and leafy. Those of the iris are petal-like and drooping and are called "falls." The most eccentric forms occur when one part of the calyx is enlarged into a

62

nectary, as in nasturtium and jewelweed. In florets of the Composite family, the calyx has shrunk into a fringe of tiny scales or hairs.

In monkshood, all the showy parts of the flower are sepals. The petals have dwindled and become the two upright nectaries. The blue protective hood is a sepal, which still does what most sepals do. But the other four act as though they were petals, attracting and guiding insects.

When sepals are united, they form an excellent protective envelope for the bud and seed. Such a calyx is tubular, like a united corolla. As a general rule, a flower with joined sepals also has joined petals.

Sometimes a calyx seems to be lacking merely because it fell off as the blossom opened. This always happens with bugbane and goldenseal. Since these flowers never have petals, they are left with only a fringe of stamens. Poppies push their sepals

UNITED SEPALS

CLOVER

SAGE

CAMPION

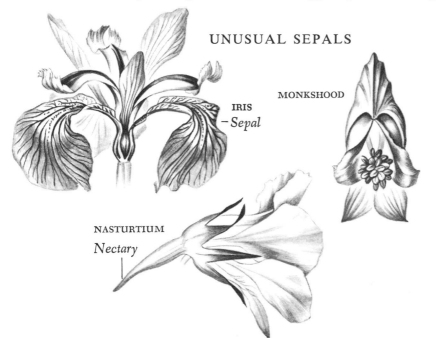

UNUSUAL SEPALS

IRIS
— *Sepal*

MONKSHOOD

NASTURTIUM
Nectary

63

over their heads as their petals unfold. In some other plants, the sepals fall when the petals and stamens do.

But most often the calyx remains until after the fruit is ripe. We can nearly always find it clinging at the stem end of a berry or hanging, brown and crumpled, below an empty seed pod.

Bracts

We have now examined the four rings of parts—pistils, stamens, petals, and sepals. These, with their receptacle, form the complete flower. But close around them we often find leafy structures which look rather like petals or sepals. These are *bracts*.

Bracts really are small leaves. They occur at many places on a plant. They nearly always grow where flower clusters branch or where each little flower stalk joins the main stem. But we are now interested only in the ones which grow close to the flowers. They can easily deceive the unwary.

We have already seen those which imitate the calyx of the pasque-flower. Others are even more confusing. They have lost their green color and have become large and showy, like a corolla. The white "petals" of dogwood and the red ones of

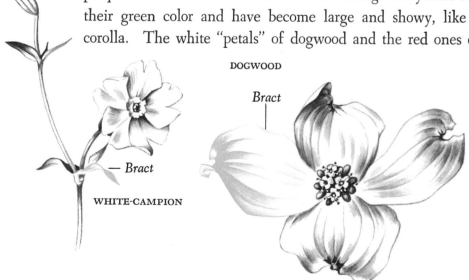

DOGWOOD

Bract

— *Bract*

WHITE-CAMPION

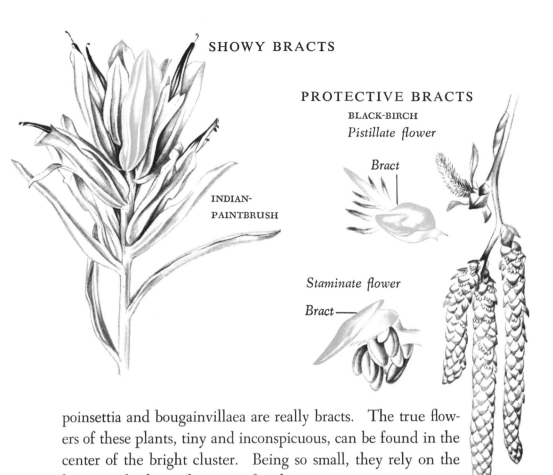

PROTECTIVE BRACTS

BLACK-BIRCH

Pistillate flower

Bract

INDIAN-
PAINTBRUSH

Staminate flower

Bract

poinsettia and bougainvillaea are really bracts. The true flowers of these plants, tiny and inconspicuous, can be found in the center of the bright cluster. Being so small, they rely on the bracts to do their advertising for them.

The eye-catching parts of Indian-paintbrush are all bracts, with the flowers concealed inside. In some tightly packed flower clusters, like those of bee-balm, clover, and heal-all, colored bracts grow among the small flowers. Thus they add to the total brightness of the head.

However, bracts are primarily designed to protect something. A bract covers each tiny floret in a tree catkin. Some of these tree flowers, like birch, bloom so early that the stamens and pistils barely poke their noses out into the cold to shed and receive pollen.

65

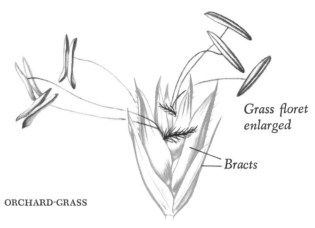

Grass floret
enlarged

Bracts

ORCHARD-GRASS

The visible parts of grass heads are nearly all bracts. And so are the big sheaths around the flower clusters of the Arum family, such as those of skunk-cabbage and jack-in-the-pulpit. Here the bract is called a *spathe*. The tiny flowers inside it bloom in very early spring and need the shelter of its tough and leathery overcoat.

Communities of Flowers

A flower with a big or bright corolla will always attract attention. But its chances of being noticed are even better if it joins with other blossoms to form a large patch of color. Only rarely can a plant risk standing alone in the woods, as the lady-slipper does, carrying a single flower on a single stem.

Most plants, even the ones with blossoms as large and bright as the tiger-lily's, group their flowers in communities or clusters. Such communities gain in both visibility and efficiency. Material is saved when one set of roots, stems, and leaves can serve many flowers. When the clusters are compact, the flowers themselves can shield and protect each other. And the insect visitor is saved much time when he finds dozens of anthers and nectar glands only a step apart.

66

Flower clusters may be loose and many-branched, like those of Saint-John's-wort and fringed-loosestrife. Or they may be small, compact heads like those of clover. But in each plant species, the flowers are arranged in a characteristic pattern (called an *inflorescence*), which never varies. These patterns are very important. They are one of the first things a botanist mentions in describing a plant.

After we have examined a great many clusters, small or large, simple or branched, pointed or flat-topped, we discover that there are really only a few basic patterns. These are shown in the illustrations and defined below:

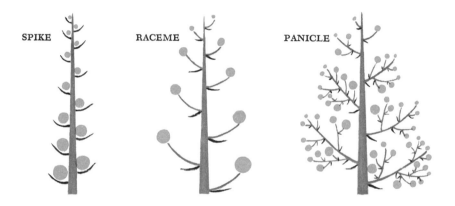

SPIKE, a single stem bearing flowers which do not have individual stalks (mullein, peppermint).

RACEME, a single stem bearing flowers which have individual stalks. The lowest stalks are usually somewhat longer than the upper ones (pokeweed, wild cherry).

PANICLE, a central stem with branches, each branch bearing stalked flowers. A panicle is thus a compound raceme (stoneroot, Canada-goldenrod).

67

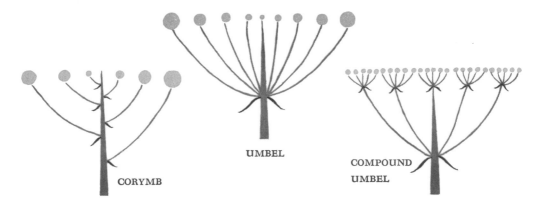

CORYMB

UMBEL

COMPOUND UMBEL

CORYMB, a modified panicle. The main stem has branches, and the outer branches are the longest, so that the cluster is flat-topped, or nearly so (yarrow, hawthorn).

UMBEL, another flat-topped cluster. The flower stalks all arise from the same point and radiate like the ribs of an umbrella. There may be smaller umbels at the tips of the radiating stalks, forming a *compound umbel* (milkweed, Queen-Anne's-lace).

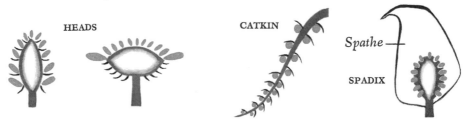

HEADS

CATKIN

Spathe

SPADIX

HEAD, a tight cluster of stalkless flowers on a very short stem or receptacle (clover, daisy).

CATKIN or *ament,* a hanging, flexible spike of very small flowers (poplar, birch).

SPADIX, a spike-like inflorescence with very small flowers embedded in a thick, fleshy stem. It is usually surrounded by a large bract, the spathe (jack-in-the-pulpit, skunk-cabbage).

68

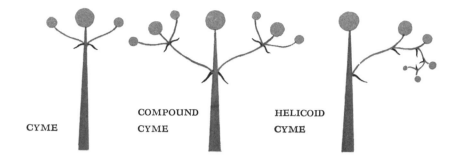

CYME   COMPOUND CYME   HELICOID CYME

CYME, a cluster, usually opposite-branched, with the oldest flower in the middle of each fork (linden, campion).

HELICOID CYME, a cyme in which the flowers on one side of each fork are missing, so that it grows in a spiral (heliotrope, sundew).

Any type of flower cluster offers some advantages, but the most efficient clusters are the most compact ones. Therefore, in many plants, evolution has produced masses of extremely tiny florets instead of large and showy blossoms.

This is especially beneficial for wind-pollinated plants. The tiny tree flowers, for instance, need the shelter they find in a catkin. They can send their pollen out in clouds a hundred times more effective than the minute puff from one set of stamens. And the pollen is caught by a cluster of pistils much more easily than by one lone stigma.

Among insect flowers too, the mass multiplies the effectiveness of each little blossom. Black-haw and elderberry bear small white flowers. But they bear them in large cymes that can be seen for a long distance. Such clusters give insects a good landing surface and a concentrated food supply. And each little floret receives the maximum of protection.

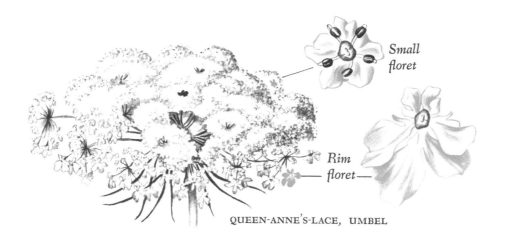

Small floret

Rim floret

QUEEN-ANNE'S-LACE, UMBEL

Flowers of the Parsley family often go one step further in efficiency. In Queen-Anne's-lace, for instance, the flat-topped umbel is made up of very small florets. Most of them are seen only as part of the mass. But the ones on the outside rim are enlarged to serve as banners. And in the very center of every white umbel, there is a single deep-purple floret—a kind of bull's-eye for the foraging insect.

In the clusters of many hydrangeas, the outer flowers have large, petal-like sepals, but no stamens or pistils. They attract

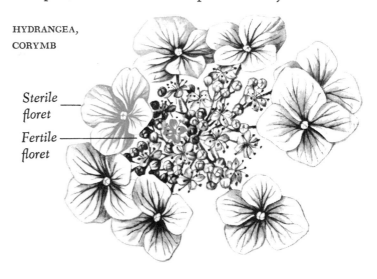

HYDRANGEA, CORYMB

Sterile floret

Fertile floret

70

insects and serve as landing places. Only the small inner flowers attend to pollen-making and seed-bearing. Thus the outer florets do what petals usually do. The cluster as a whole carries out the functions of a single flower, dividing up the duties of seed-making and attraction.

This trend reaches its climax in the Composite family. The name comes from the fact that each cluster, or head, is composed of many tiny florets. And the head not only acts like a single flower but even looks like one.

The common sunflower—a typical composite—bears heads which most people quite understandably mistake for flowers. The dark circle in the center looks like a mass of pistils and stamens. But it is really a tight-packed group of tiny but complete tubular flowers. They are called *disk florets.* Encircling them is a ring of yellow "petals." Each bright banner—called a *ray*—is the corolla of an individual flower. Disk florets and ray florets both grow from the top of a flat receptacle or *disk.* Enclosing the disk is the *involucre,* a sheath of green bracts which looks much like a calyx.

SUNFLOWER, HEAD

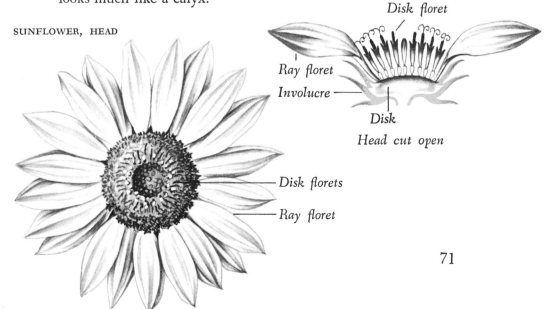

Disk floret

Ray floret

Involucre

Disk

Head cut open

Disk florets

Ray floret

71

In operation, this head is like an extremely efficient single flower. The mass of disk florets devotes itself entirely to making seeds. Anything else it does is quite incidental. But sometimes, simply because of its color contrast, it serves as a target for insects.

By itself, a disk floret is anything but conspicuous. Its corolla is merely a tube to contain stamens and stigma, above an ovary which produces one big seed. In the closely packed head, a protective calyx is no longer needed, so it has disappeared. Some botanists think that the two tiny scales at the top of the ovary are the remains of sepals. In other composites, this leftover calyx, or *pappus,* is a ring of hairs. It expands later and becomes the well-known seed parachute of such plants as dandelion and goat's-beard.

Ray florets are primarily attention getters. Quite often, as in the sunflower, they have lost the power of producing seeds. In cases where they are still fertile, they have ovaries, pappus, and pistils like those of the disk florets, but no stamens. The corolla is their most important part. It is straplike in shape, resembling a tube which has been slit open and flattened out.

The involucre serves as a kind of compound calyx. It is usually green. Its small bracts lie in rows and often overlap

Disk, or tube, floret

Fertile

Ray, or strap, florets

Sterile

HEAD OF ASTER

UNOPENED HEAD OF SUNFLOWER

INVOLUCRES

like shingles. It encloses the unopened head like a bud and later shelters the growing seeds. The involucre can vary in shape from the flat saucer of sunflower and daisy to the narrow cup of boneset. Sometimes, as in cocklebur, it is covered with spines and acts as another kind of seed distributor.

BONESET

The advantages of heads like these are obvious. Material is saved, pollination of all florets is almost certain, and seed protection is excellent. Composites reproduce themselves in immense numbers. In late summer and fall, they nearly take over the floral stage. Even unbotanical poets regard "goldenrod and asters" as symbols of the autumn season.

COCKLEBUR

The other really big plant family of the temperate zone also owes its success to compact floral communities. These are the wind-pollinated grasses. They are very different from composites, chiefly because of their partnership with wind instead of insects. When their tiny flowers are grouped in heads, it is not for advertising, but for economy and protection. So they have lost all the parts which normally make flowers conspicuous.

The individual florets of grasses are almost microscopic, and it is hard to study them. Besides, they do not look like flowers. They have neither corolla nor calyx. And their pistils and stamens are almost concealed by scalelike bracts. But with the help of a lens and a little patience we can discover that the head of a grass is as efficient as that of a composite. And, in its delicate way, it is sometimes as beautiful.

Most of us are familiar with the flower clusters of grasses—feathery panicles or simple spikes. Within these we find the part which corresponds to the head of a composite—the *spikelet*. Each spikelet may be composed of a great many florets or a very few or only one.

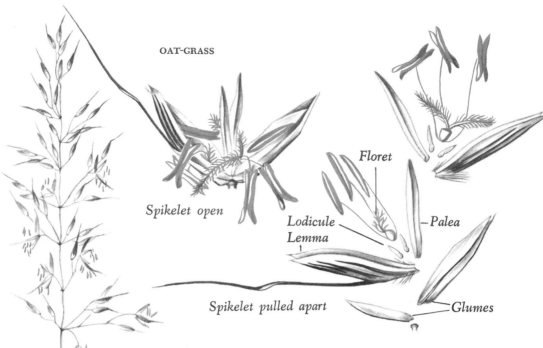

Floret

Spikelet open

Lodicule
Lemma

Palea

Spikelet pulled apart

Glumes

The spikelets of oat-grass grow in a delicate panicle. Each spikelet has two florets. We can see their parts only after we have pulled them apart with a pin.

Starting at the base of a spikelet, we find first two transparent scales, or *glumes*. These are bracts, which protect the whole spikelet. The next two scales enclose a floret and are called *flowering scales*. The outer, larger, one is the *lemma*. The inner, smaller, one is the *palea*.

Inside them, at the base of the floret, are two minute white scales called *lodicules*. They are all that remain of the corolla. We can scarcely see them except at blooming time, when they swell with liquid and push open the stiff flowering scales. Some grasses do not have lodicules. Their spikelets never open, and stamens and pistils have to squeeze out at the tips of the palea and lemma.

The floret itself is nothing but a pistil and three stamens—

74

a typical grass flower. The anthers are big. The filaments are long and threadlike. The two feathery stigma arms spread out above a simple egg-shaped ovary.

The ovary of each flower produces only one seed. But the seed is wonderfully rich in nutriment. And it is often equipped, like those of composites, with devices to aid in distribution. However, in this case, the hooks or bristles or hairs are on the protective scales rather than on the seed itself.

Grasses, too, have profited from grouping their flowers in communities. The family is the most widespread in the vegetable kingdom—"of all common plants, the most common."

Spikelet with bristle

Seed

Monocots and Dicots

All this information about the basic structure of plants is necessary for any present-day botanist who intends to classify them. The variations in structure were arrived at through long evolution. They are the key to plant relationships. Knowing about them, we are ready to meet a few important families.

But first we should be acquainted with the two large groups into which all flowering plants are divided. These groups are very important and very easy to tell apart. Even their names—*Monocotyledons* and *Dicotyledons*—are not hard when we understand what they mean.

When a bean seed starts to grow, it sends down a root and sends up a stem. The main body of the seed splits into two parts, which are called *seed leaves* or *cotyledons*. Since there are two of them, the bean plant is known as a Dicotyledon, which we commonly shorten to "dicot." Other plants have only one seed leaf and are called Monocotyledons, or monocots.

These two groups have evolved separately for millions of years. Each has some primitive members as well as some very highly developed ones.

The number of seed leaves is a basic difference between the two groups, but there are other important differences. The monocots, which include plants like lilies, grasses, and orchids, commonly have these characteristics:

1. *One seed leaf*
2. *Number plans of three*
3. *Petals and sepals which look alike*
4. *Leaves simple, usually not toothed*
5. *Leaves with parallel veins*
6. *Stems all or partly underground (in the form of bulbs, rhizomes, etc.)*
7. *Stem, when above ground, seldom much branched*
8. *Mostly low plants; tree forms rare*

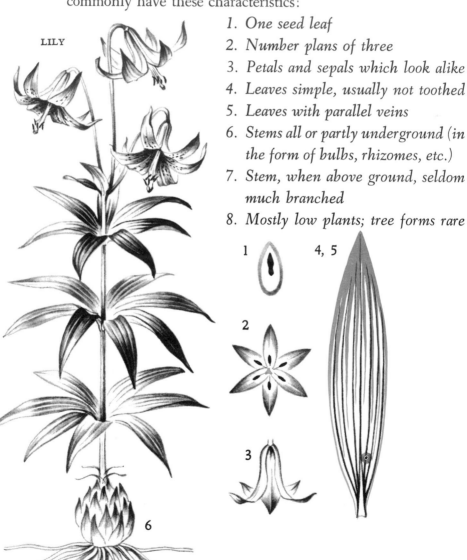

LILY

The dicots are by far the larger and more varied group. They can be as different as a violet and an oak tree. Their general characteristics are:

1. *Two seed leaves*
2. *Number plans of four or five*
3. *Petals and sepals distinct and recognizable*
4. *Leaves simple or compound, of every conceivable shape, toothed or smooth-edged*
5. *Leaves with a radiating network of veins*
6. *Stems without underground bulbs*
7. *Stems short or tall; often much branched*
8. *Many tree forms*

GERANIUM

1

2

3

4, 5

6

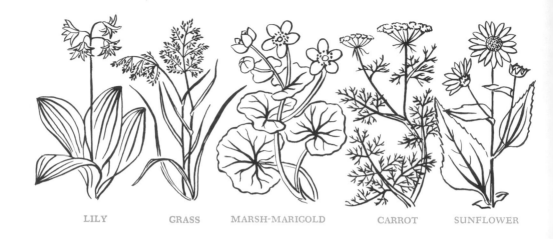

LILY GRASS MARSH-MARIGOLD CARROT SUNFLOWER

Plant Families

There are about three hundred families of flowering plants in the world. It takes many years to get acquainted with all of them. But some families are very common in garden or countryside. And some of these are very easily recognized.

We are going to introduce you to ten common families. Knowing them will enable you to recognize and identify a large number of our everyday plants. And it will give you an idea of what family relationships are like. It will also be a stepping stone to the study of other families.

The key to these family relationships is provided by the flower parts, which we have examined in previous chapters. Floral structure is the most significant characteristic of a plant, and it varies much less than other characteristics do. For instance, the flowers of a locust tree, a bean vine, and a small clover plant show us that the three are closely related. In spite of their different ways of growth, they belong to the same family.

78

Of our ten common families, more than half are highly evolved, with elaborate pollination mechanisms. This is, of course, to be expected. They have become common because they were well equipped to survive.

As much as possible, flowers should be studied right on the spot where they grow. If you very much want to examine small structures at home, pick a few blossoms and enclose them tightly in a plastic bag. But do this only when there are plenty of them. *Never* pick a flower when there is only one of the kind (or even two or three). If you love it enough to study it, you do not want to help destroy the species.

The following families are arranged approximately in order of evolution. In general, flowers with many parts are more primitive than those with few parts. Separate parts are less advanced than united ones.

LILY FAMILY—Liliaceae (*Monocot*)

This large family is found all over the world, especially in warm and tropical regions. It is the most typical monocot family, and many botanists consider it very close to the type of plant from which all monocots developed. The group as a whole is easily recognized, except for a few unusual cases. These are so different from the type that they are sometimes separated into families of their own.

The whole family is insect pollinated, so most of its members have showy flowers. Everyone knows the beautiful garden "ornamentals": lily, tulip, hyacinth, trillium, lily-of-the-valley. And everyone has eaten onion, leek, garlic, and asparagus. We get medicines from many members of the family: squill, false-

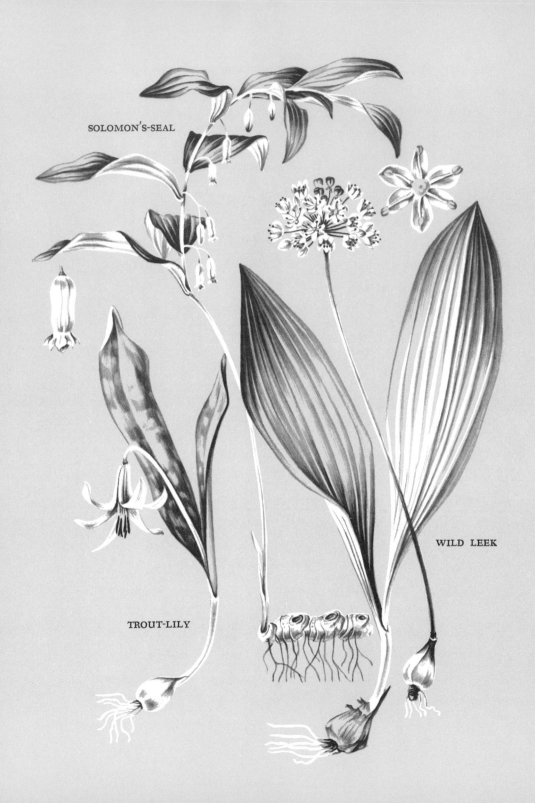

SOLOMON'S-SEAL

WILD LEEK

TROUT-LILY

hellebore, autumn-crocus. Yucca roots have been used for soap, sansevieria for fiber, and aloes for embalming. In the country, the family includes some of our loveliest wild flowers: trout-lily, Canada-lily, Solomon's-seal, bellwort.

1, 3, 5

GENERAL CHARACTERISTICS (*of the family as a whole, not of any particular species*):

2

1. The typical flower has three sepals and three petals, which all look very much alike. All six are called *perianth segments* or, sometimes, *tepals*.

2. The perianth segments are always regular. Usually they are separate, but occasionally are united into a tubular corolla.

4

3. There are six stamens.

4. There is one pistil, with three united carpels.

5. The ovary is superior.

6. The fruit is usually a capsule with many seeds. Occasionally it is a berry.

7. The leaves often have a sheathlike base which wraps around the stem of the plant.

6

SOLOMON'S-
SEAL

GARLIC

MARIPOSA-
LILY

GRASS FAMILY—Gramineae (*Monocot*)

The Latin name of this family means simply "grasses." It is an extremely large group. In fact, if we consider the number of individual plants rather than the number of species, it is the largest family on earth. And it is by far the most useful to man, so useful that his early development was always closely tied to the grasslands. There he found pasture for his animals and staple food for himself.

All the grains we eat are grass seeds. A great part of our sugar comes from a grass—sugar-cane. Bamboo is a grass, used for everything from building houses to making clothing. Other members of the family furnish medicines, alcoholic drinks, oil, and insulation.

Grasses are valuable for their ability to hold the surface of the earth in place. Their tangle of roots and stems forms a net. This keeps the topsoil of our prairies from drying up and blowing away, reclaims marshes, and ties down sand dunes.

Grasses have evolved a long way from the original monocots. They are a highly developed family, which accounts for their tremendous success.

Except for a few self-pollinated ones, grasses are all wind pollinated. Their flowers are almost perfect in their adaptation to this method. The parts are so reduced in number and size that we can scarcely recognize them. Very little is left except the basic essentials—stamens to produce clouds of pollen, and pistils to catch that pollen and then produce seeds. Grass flowers usually open early in the morning, often for the briefest possible time. A wheat flower, for instance, is open only about fifteen minutes.

82

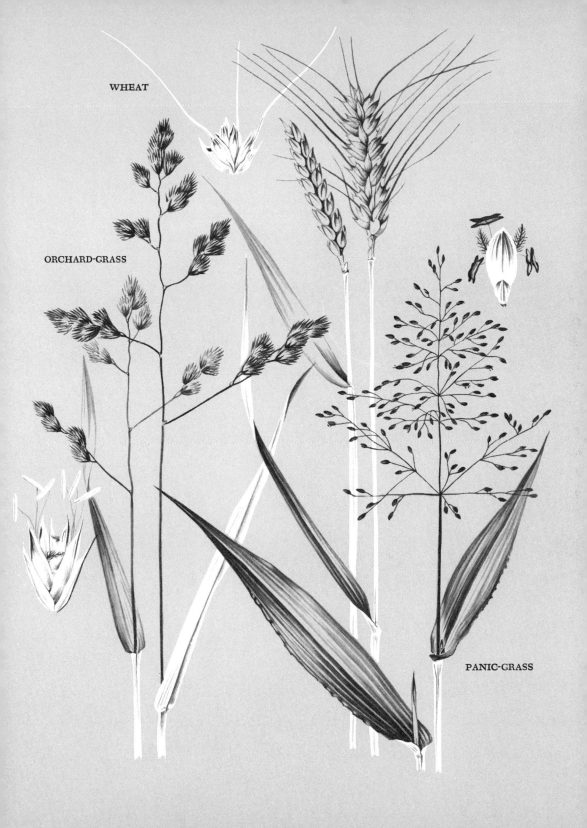

WHEAT

ORCHARD-GRASS

PANIC-GRASS

A typical grass flower is described in detail on pages 74-75.

GENERAL CHARACTERISTICS:

Grass flowers are so small that they cannot be seen clearly without a hand lens. But if they are pulled apart with a pin and examined through a lens, they are not hard to understand.

1. The tiny flowers, or florets, are grouped in spikelets. The spikelets are grouped in spikes or panicles.

2. Each spikelet is enclosed by two bracts, called glumes.

3. Inside the spikelet, each floret is enclosed by two bracts —a palea and a lemma.

4. Petals and sepals have almost disappeared. They are represented by two or three minute lodicules. These lodicules swell and push open the palea and lemma to expose the anthers and stigma. Some flowers, without lodicules, do not open.

5. Stamens are usually three, with long slender filaments.

6. The pistil has one carpel with one ovule, and, usually, two feathery stigmas.

7. The fruit is a grain or nutlet.

8. Leaves are commonly long and narrow, with sheaths that wrap around the stem (see page 83).

9. Stems are round and hollow, with prominent joints.

ORCHID FAMILY—Orchidaceae (*Monocot*)

To those of us who live in the United States, orchids seem rare and exotic. Actually they are anything but rare, since the family is one of the largest in the world. Most orchids, however, grow in the tropics. The jungle is the original home of all the species we see in florists' shops. They are conspicuous in color and fantastic in shape because they have to compete with a dense mass of vegetation in order to be pollinated. They are usually found growing on trees, but are not parasitic.

There are, however, large numbers of orchids growing in our own woods, fields, and—especially—swamps: lady-slipper, helleborine, calypso, ladies'-tresses. They face less competition than their tropical cousins, and are consequently smaller and less conspicuous. Since they grow on the ground, they are called "terrestrial orchids."

These beautiful and complicated flowers are the most highly developed of the monocots. With parts often enlarged or ruffled or twisted, they seem difficult to understand.

First and most important, there is in the center of every orchid a projecting, irregular structure. This is called the *column*. It is merely the pistil and stamens united into one body. The

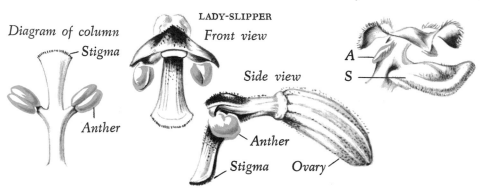

Diagram of column
— Stigma
Anther

LADY-SLIPPER
Front view

Side view
Anther
Stigma   Ovary

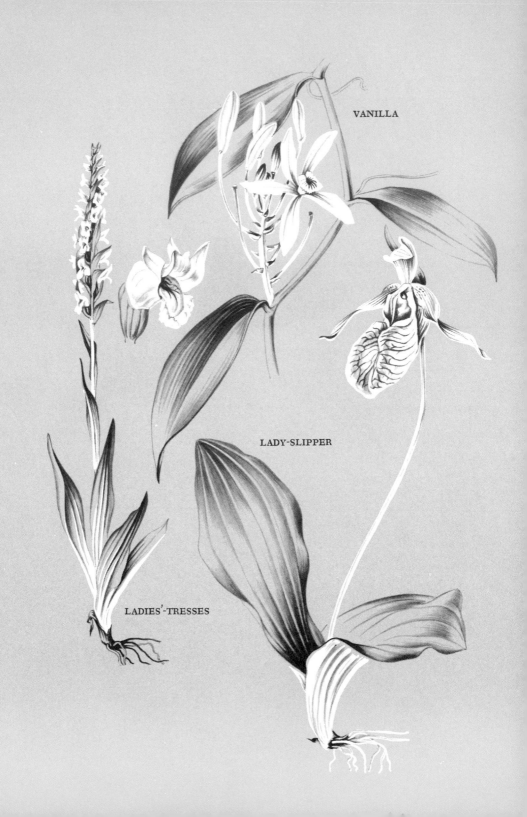

VANILLA

LADY-SLIPPER

LADIES'-TRESSES

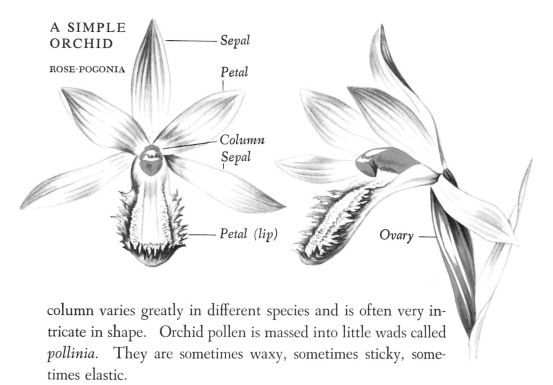

A SIMPLE
ORCHID

ROSE-POGONIA

Sepal

Petal

Column

Sepal

Petal (lip)

Ovary

column varies greatly in different species and is often very intricate in shape. Orchid pollen is massed into little wads called *pollinia*. They are sometimes waxy, sometimes sticky, sometimes elastic.

The other parts of the orchid are easier to recognize. There are three petals. One is usually enlarged in some way, like the pouch of the lady-slipper, and is called the *lip*. The three sepals are often brightly colored. And often, like the sepals of their lily ancestors, they look much like the petals.

Orchids have most remarkable devices for pollination. In various ways the insect is coaxed into contact with the pollinia. They stick tightly to his head or tongue or body. Then, as he flies away, they are pulled out of their anther pouches and carried on to the stigmas of other flowers.

The orchid family has very few uses outside of ornamentation. Some members provide medicines: coralroot, lady-slipper. And the seed pod of one is the source of vanilla.

87

Orchids are difficult to raise outside the tropics. The species which grow on other plants have roots and leaves especially adapted for this kind of life. And all orchids depend for at least part of their food on the cooperation of a special kind of fungus which grows at their roots. Their thousands of tiny seeds have no built-in protection or food supply, so they must sprout very quickly or not at all.

GENERAL CHARACTERISTICS:

1. The flowers are very irregular.

2. Usually neither sepals nor petals are united.

HELLEBORINE

3. The three sepals are shaped, and often colored, like petals. In lady-slipper, the two lower ones are joined.

4. There are three petals, one enlarged, ruffled, or pouch-shaped, and called the lip. The lip often bears a nectar spur.

5. There are one or two stamens, united with the pistil in a column. The pollen is in the form of pollinia.

6. The pistil has an inferior ovary with three carpels. Its style and stigma are part of the column.

7. The fruit is a capsule with innumerable seeds.

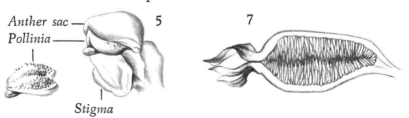

Anther sac —
Pollinia ——
5
7
Stigma

BUTTERCUP FAMILY—Ranunculaceae
(Dicot)

This large family includes some of our best-loved wild flowers: anemone, columbine, larkspur, buttercup. The Latin name means "little frog" and comes from the fact that a few of the best known members grow in wet places: marsh-marigold, swamp-buttercup. But the greatest number are forest dwellers, very abundant in the woods of North America. Mostly, they bloom in early spring, before the trees have enough leaves to shut out the sun. And most are rather small and tender. Only clematis grows into a vine.

None of the members of the family are commonly eaten. Their juice is acrid and even poisonous, and several are used for medicine: monkshood, goldenseal, pasque-flower, bugbane. Goldthread has yellow roots which yield a dye. But it is in our gardens that the family really shines, because of its variety and beauty of form. Some flowers have curiously shaped petals or sepals: columbine, monkshood, larkspur. Others have peculiar staminodes: Christmas-rose, goldthread.

This group is considered a very old family. Its simpler members may be very close to the primitive type from which both dicots and monocots have sprung.

The flowers are nearly all insect pollinated. Some, like buttercup and anemone, are very simple in the arrangement of their parts, with no special devices for guiding insects.

Others have developed a variety of curious shapes fitted to special pollinizers. Monkshood can be pollinated only by bumblebees and therefore grows only where bumblebees live.

CLEMATIS

HEPATICA

BUTTERCUP

90

The nectar in a columbine's long spurs is beyond the reach of all but long-tongued insects. Meadow-rue is wind pollinated and has completely lost its petals.

1, 3, 4

GENERAL CHARACTERISTICS:

1. There are three to fifteen sepals, always separate and usually regular in arrangement.

2. The petals match the sepals in number. They too are always separate and usually regular.

3. In some species, the petals are missing and are replaced by petal-like sepals: anemone, hepatica. In others, the sepals, too, seem to be missing, because they fall off as the flower opens: baneberry, bugbane.

4. There are many separate stamens.

5. There are usually many separate pistils, each with a single carpel.

6. The ovaries are always superior.

7. The fruit is most often a dry pod. But in some species it is a berry, and in others it is a one-seeded hard fruit called an *achene*.

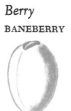

Berry
BANEBERRY

Pod
HELLEBORE

Achenes
CLEMATIS
BUTTERCUP

MUSTARD FAMILY—Cruciferae (*Dicot*)

This family name comes from two Latin words meaning "crossbearers." The flowers have four petals arranged in the form of a Maltese cross, so they are very easily recognized. In fact, flowers of the whole family are so much alike that it is difficult to separate one from another. This can be done only by studying other parts, such as seed pods, seeds, and plant hairs.

We know the family best through its edible members: mustard, radish, turnip, water-cress, cabbage, cauliflower. But it also includes a large number of our commonest wild flowers: winter-cress, shepherd's-purse, penny-cress, wallflower. Many have been "weeds" since prehistoric times and have followed the development of agriculture over Europe and America.

An old-fashioned garden is full of crucifers: sweet-alyssum, sweet-rocket, candytuft, honesty. Mustard is the only medicinal member; but rape furnishes oil, and woad gives a blue dye.

The whole family has nectar, and most species are insect pollinated. A few pollinate themselves.

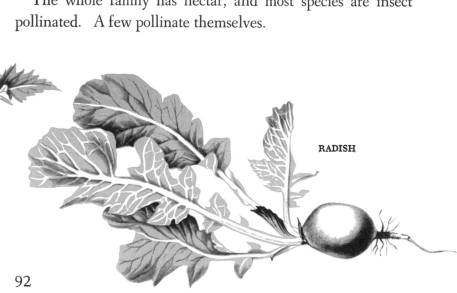

RADISH

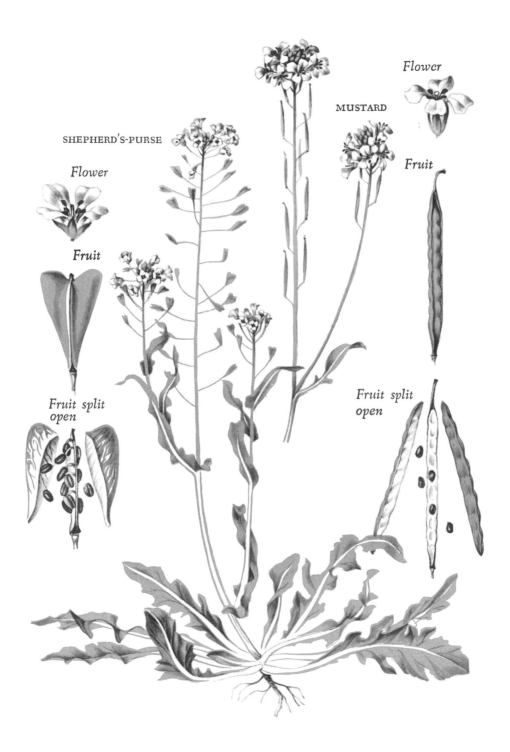

SHEPHERD'S-PURSE

Flower

Fruit

*Fruit split
open*

MUSTARD

Flower

Fruit

*Fruit split
open*

GENERAL CHARACTERISTICS:

1. Flowers always grow in clusters (a corymb, which gradually elongates and leaves the seed pods behind in a long raceme) (see page 93).

2. The calyx is formed of four green sepals. They are separate, but appear to be united because they overlap.

3. The four petals are separate. They often have a long, tapering base, or *claw*.

4. There are six stamens, four long and two short.

5. The pistil has a superior ovary with two carpels.

6. The fruit is a kind of capsule called a *silique* or, when very short, a *silicle*. Its two halves are separated by a thin wall. The ripe fruit usually splits open in two halves, with the central wall still in between, holding the seeds. These capsules vary in shape and are the best key to identification of the different species.

7. The plants often have a rosette of leaves at the base, as well as leaves on the stem (see page 93).

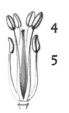

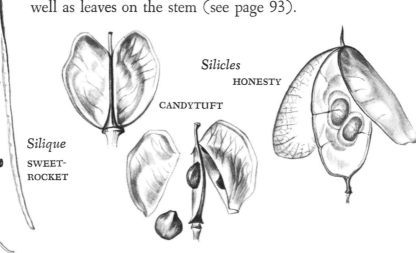

Silicles
HONESTY

CANDYTUFT

Silique
SWEET-
ROCKET

WILD ROSE

ROSE FAMILY—Rosaceae (*Dicot*)

This large family is found in all parts of the world, but especially in the northern temperate regions. It varies so much that some botanists think it should be split up into several families.

Roses are probably the best known and best loved of all garden flowers. But, though they have given their name to the family, they form only a very small part of it. Much more important to man are the fruit-bearing trees: apple, pear, cherry, plum, peach; and the berry-covered vines: strawberry, blackberry, raspberry. Almond fruits look much like apricots, but their seed is the nut we eat. Rose fruits (hips) are edible and were used in England during World War II as a valuable source of vitamin C.

Medicines are derived from a number of the plants in this family: almond, wild-cherry, peach, blackberry. The leaves of burnet are a delicate addition to salads. And the wood of some trees—cherry, apple—is valuable for furniture and engraving.

Our gardens and countrysides are full of beautiful members of the family, in addition to roses. The trees include haw-

BURNET

HAWTHORN

CINQUEFOIL

96

thorn, mountain-ash, shad-bush. The shrubs, spiraea, coton-easter, fire-thorn. The herbs, agrimony, cinquefoil, avens.

Nearly all are insect pollinated. They have showy flowers and abundant pollen, though not all have nectar (roses don't). Burnet is wind pollinated and has no corolla.

GENERAL CHARACTERISTICS:

1. The calyx has five separate sepals. They are green and often leaflike.

2. There are five free petals, in a regular circle. (Garden roses have been "doubled" by horticulturists.)

3. There are usually a great many stamens, arranged in rings of five.

4. The pistils vary from one to a great many, most often with separate carpels.

5. The most important variations are in the fruits and in the way the flower parts are arranged on the receptacle:

   a. *Spiraea.* The receptacle is saucer-shaped, with the parts all attached on top of it. The pistils develop into separate dry seed capsules.

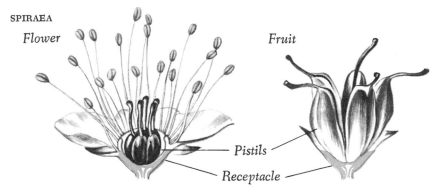

SPIRAEA

Flower

Fruit

Pistils

Receptacle

Flower

Fruit

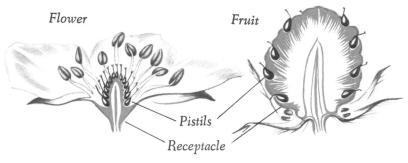

Pistils

Receptacle

b. *Strawberry, avens, blackberry.* The receptacle is a mound or cone with the pistils on it. Sepals, petals, and stamens are attached around its base. The true fruit is a small seed. The edible part of the strawberry is the enlarged receptacle, with the seeds on its surface.

c. *Cherry, plum, peach.* The receptacle is cuplike, with a wide opening. The pistil is attached at the bottom of the cup. The other parts are attached to the rim of the cup. The ovary becomes the part we eat—a type of fruit called a *drupe*.

WILD CHERRY

Flower

Fruit

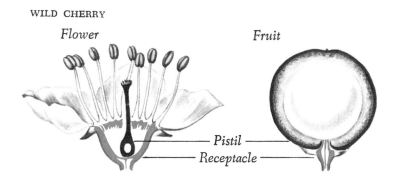

Pistil
Receptacle

98

Flower   *Fruit*

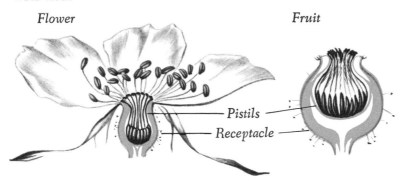

— *Pistils*
— *Receptacle*

d. *Rose.* The receptacle is cup-shaped with a very small opening. The pistils are inside the cup. The other parts are attached to its rim. Rose hips are the receptacle, with the fruits inside.

e. *Apple, pear, hawthorn.* The receptacle is closed over the top, completely surrounding the ovary and merging with it. We eat the receptacle, throw away the "core," which is the ovary and seeds.

APPLE

Flower   *Fruit*

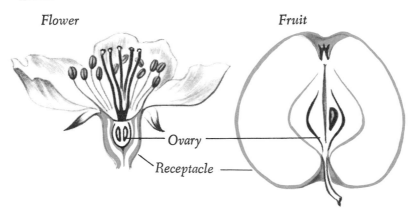

— *Ovary* —
Receptacle —

99

GARDEN PEA

PEA FAMILY—Fabaceae (*Dicot*)

This family has already been split off from a larger group. It used to be considered part of a very big family called Leguminosae, and it is still listed that way in many books. "Fabaceae" comes from a Greek word meaning "to eat."

Its members are very easy to recognize, with their "butterfly"-shaped flowers. Some are trees: locust, sandalwood; some are vines: wisteria, bean, vetch; some are herbs: clover, lupine. Many are ornamental: sweet-pea, wisteria. And hundreds have economic value. We eat the protein-rich seeds of several of them: peas, beans, lentils, peanuts.

Some are poisonous to eat: broom, loco. A very large number produce drugs: licorice, sweet-clover, fenugreek, calabar-bean. Several yield dyes: indigo, genista, sandalwood; some yield timber: rosewood. Soya-beans furnish fodder, oils, and raw material for plastics. Alfalfa and clover are food for animals. Among the wild species are tick-trefoil, golden-pea, and ground-nut with its edible tubers.

100

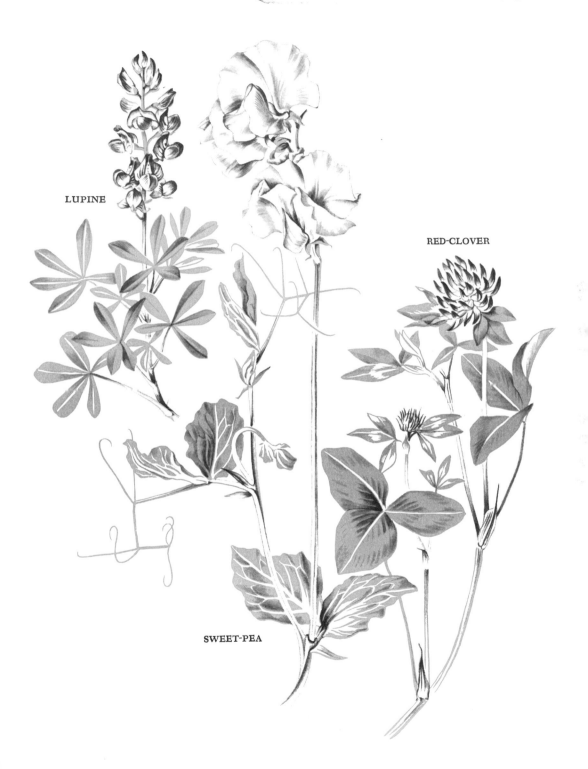

LUPINE

RED-CLOVER

SWEET-PEA

Most members of the family have on their roots small nodules containing nitrogen-fixing bacteria. The bacteria find protection in the nodules and the plants benefit from the nitrogen. Because of this characteristic, some members of the pea family are used as "green fertilizer." They are plowed into the ground to provide nitrogen for other plants.

Pea flowers always have a very distinctive shape, with their five irregular petals. The uppermost—the *standard*—is large and showy. It serves as a banner for insects and, with lines or spots, guides them to the nectar. The two side petals are called *wings*. The two lowest petals are always more or less united. They form the *keel* and enclose the stamens and pistil.

They do this so tightly that, in some cases, no insect can get in at all. Then the flower has to pollinate itself. But many pea flowers have a trigger device which releases the stamens suddenly and bombards the visiting bee. Sometimes the weight of a heavy bumblebee landing on the keel sets off the trigger. Sometimes an insect's tongue, thrust in at the throat of the flower, makes the stamens and pistil snap out. (We too can set off these mechanisms with a pin.)

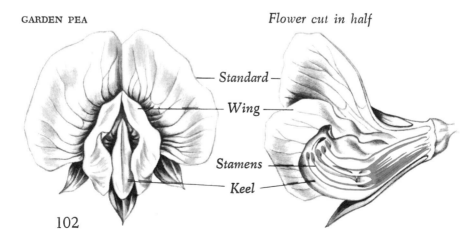

GARDEN PEA   *Flower cut in half*

— Standard —

— Wing —

Stamens —

— Keel —

102

GENERAL CHARACTERISTICS:

1. Flowers are grouped into racemes or heads.

2. The calyx is tubular, with five lobes.

2

3. The corolla is butterfly-shaped (*papilionaceous*). It has five separate petals: the uppermost is large and showy, the standard. The two side petals are the wings. The two lowest, more or less united, form the keel.

4. Inside the keel, there are usually ten stamens, with their filaments joined into a tube. Sometimes one stamen remains separate, and occasionally all the filaments are separate.

4

5. The pistil is simple, with one carpel. It contains a number of ovules.

5

6. The fruit is an important characteristic of the family. It is a pod which splits into two separate halves. In a few species, the pods do not split, but break up into sections.

7. Most of the plants have compound leaves. Often, some of the leaflets are changed into tendrils for climbing.

6

TICK-TREFOIL

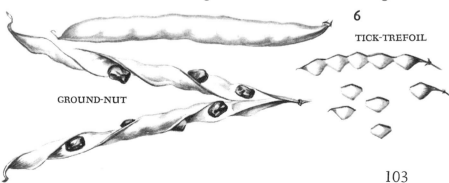

GROUND-NUT

103

PARSLEY FAMILY—Umbelliferae (*Dicot*)

This Latin name means "umbel-bearers," because the flowers grow in very distinct flat-topped umbels. These clusters, with their tiny florets, are always easy to recognize. Like the crucifers, the whole family when in flower is so much alike that species can be best identified by their fruits.

The family is plentiful all over the world, except in the tropics. Some of our commonest vegetables belong to it: parsley, carrot, parsnip, celery. Its aromatic oils have very pronounced flavors, and many are included on the kitchen spice shelf: dill, caraway, anise, chervil, fennel. However, several are dangerously poisonous to eat. Poison-hemlock was used to execute Socrates, and our own wild-parsnip and fool's-parsley could easily kill us. So we should never risk sampling them, in spite of their pleasant and tempting odors. Several are used for medicine: fennel, angelica, ferula, coriander.

In gardens, the parsley family is usually restricted to the herb and vegetable beds. But some members are large and beautiful: angelica, cow-parsnip. Golden-Alexanders is a common and attractive spring wild flower. But Queen-Anne's-lace is probably the best known of all. It is a wild form of the garden carrot. Its delicate white blossoms would be considered beautiful enough for any flower garden if it were not such a common "weed."

Pollination is accomplished by insects. The flowers are often minute, but their massed clusters are showy. The outer florets are often enlarged and sterile, serving only as banners to guide insects.

104

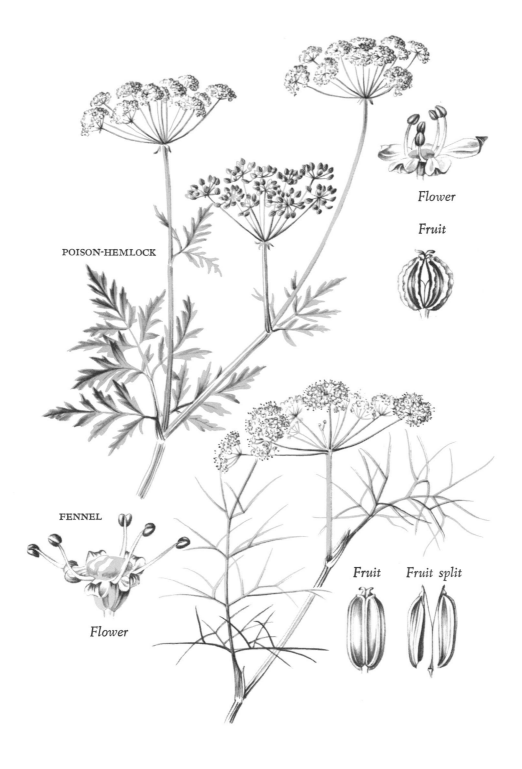

POISON-HEMLOCK

Flower

Fruit

FENNEL

Flower

Fruit   *Fruit split*

3, 4

GENERAL CHARACTERISTICS:

1. The flowers are very small, in umbels.

2. The sepals are tiny or lacking.

3. There are five free petals, each curved in at the tip.

5

4. The five stamens are attached to a disk around the base of the styles.

5. The pistil has two styles and stigmas. Its ovary is inferior, with two carpels.

6. The fruit is distinctive: The two dry carpels split apart. They separate at the base, but hang by their tops from a slender stalk. Each contains one seed. On their surfaces are the oil ducts which give the flavor.

6

7. The leaf stalks often have sheaths which wrap around the plant stems (see page 105, fennel).

8. Usually the leaves are much-divided, even fernlike.

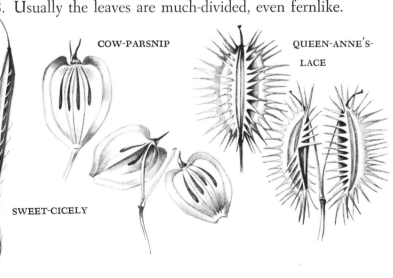

COW-PARSNIP

QUEEN-ANNE'S-
LACE

SWEET-CICELY

PENNYROYAL

MINT FAMILY—Labiatae (*Dicot*)

The name of this family comes from the Latin word *labium*, meaning "lip," and it refers to the shape of the flowers. Their tubular corollas are nearly always more or less two-lipped. This flower form, along with square stems and often scented leaves, makes the family easy to recognize.

Because of their scent, many mints are familiar to everyone: peppermint, spearmint, sage, thyme, lavender. The pungent odor comes from tiny glands on the stem and leaves, which secrete aromatic oils.

The family is especially abundant in the Mediterranean region, but it is found all over the world. Some species always grew in North America: bergamot, stoneroot; but many of our mints were brought from Europe by colonists for their herb gardens. Some of these are still seen only in gardens, but many have "escaped" and become common wild flowers here: heal-all, motherwort, ground-ivy, catnip.

More than half of our kitchen flavorings come from the members of this family. Many mints also yield medicines: horehound, catnip, skullcap, lemon-balm.

The flowers are all insect pollinated, with highly developed

107

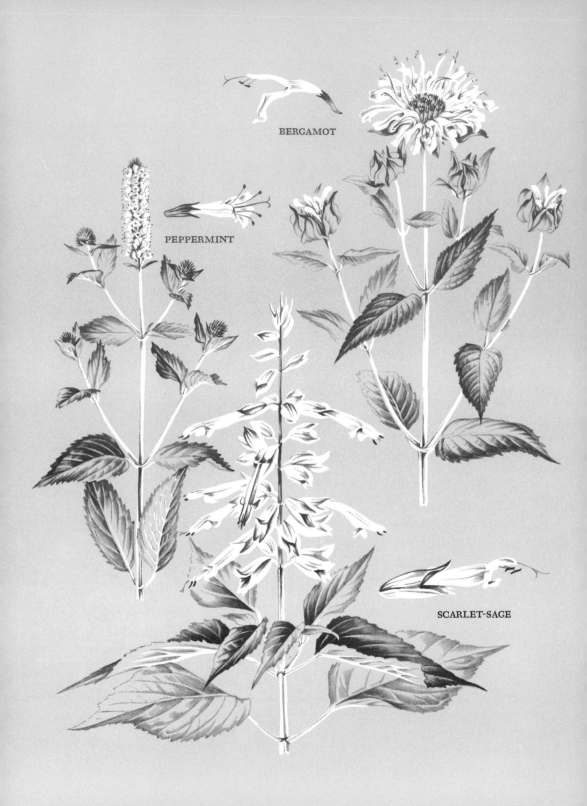

BERGAMOT

PEPPERMINT

SCARLET-SAGE

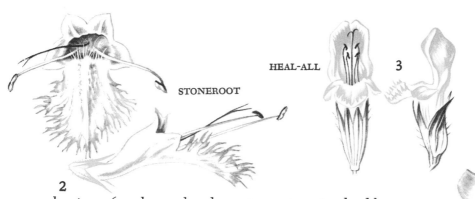

HEAL-ALL **3**

STONEROOT

2

mechanisms (we have already met one type in the blue-sage, page 25). Nectar is secreted on the disk in such large amounts that, in upright flowers, it nearly fills the corolla tube. **4**

GENERAL CHARACTERISTICS:

1. The flowers are usually small and are borne in various kinds of clusters.

2. The calyx is tubular, with five lobes or two lips.

3. The corolla is tubular. It usually has an upper lip composed of two lobes, a lower lip of three lobes.

4. There are four stamens, their filaments attached to the inside of the corolla wall. A few mints have only two stamens, often with tiny remnants of the other two. **5**

5. The pistil has a long style with a forked stigma. Its ovary has four compartments, each with one ovule.

6. Around the base of the ovary is a fleshy ring—the *disk*, which secretes nectar. **6**

7

7. The fruit type is the same in all mints: the ripened ovary splits into four one-seeded nutlets.

8. The plant has square stems.

109

COMPOSITE FAMILY—Compositae (*Dicot*)

This is one of the largest and most flourishing of all plant families. It is to the temperate regions what orchids are to the tropics. As the most highly evolved of dicots, it has many characteristics which help it to survive and spread. The compact flower heads—which give the family its name—are composed of small, closely packed florets. They are easy to pollinate and they produce quantities of seeds. These seeds are scattered by many specialized devices. And they are so sturdy and so full of nourishment that nearly all of them sprout.

The composites are a family of the sunny fields. Most of our species are fairly big. Many spend the whole summer growing and bloom only in the fall: goldenrod, aster, Joe-Pye-weed. But a few appear in earliest spring: colt's-foot, pussy-toes. Dandelion, yarrow, fleabane, and chicory bloom almost all summer long.

Such a large family, distributed all over the world, has of course, many valuable members. Our gardens are full of them: daisy, zinnia, dahlia, bachelor's-button, chrysanthemum. We eat the leaves of lettuce and chicory, the roots of oyster-plant and Jerusalem-artichoke, the flower heads of true artichoke.

Several furnish medicines: dandelion, wormwood, arnica, elecampane, tansy, camomile. Oil is made from sunflower seeds, and insect poison from a kind of daisy. Several, with milky juice, were studied in wartime as possible sources of latex, a substitute for rubber. Ragweed, unfortunately, causes hay fever.

The structure of one typical member of the family—sunflower —has already been described (page 71). However, not all

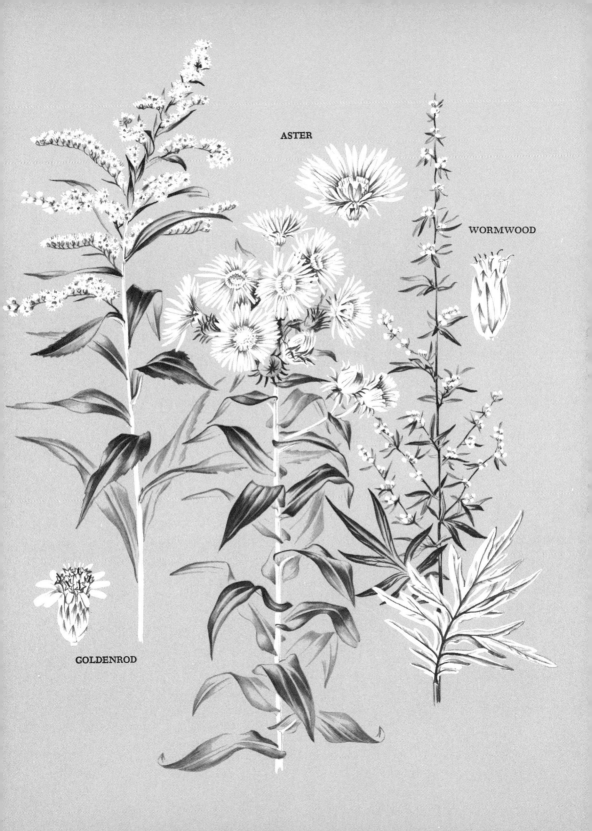

ASTER

WORMWOOD

GOLDENROD

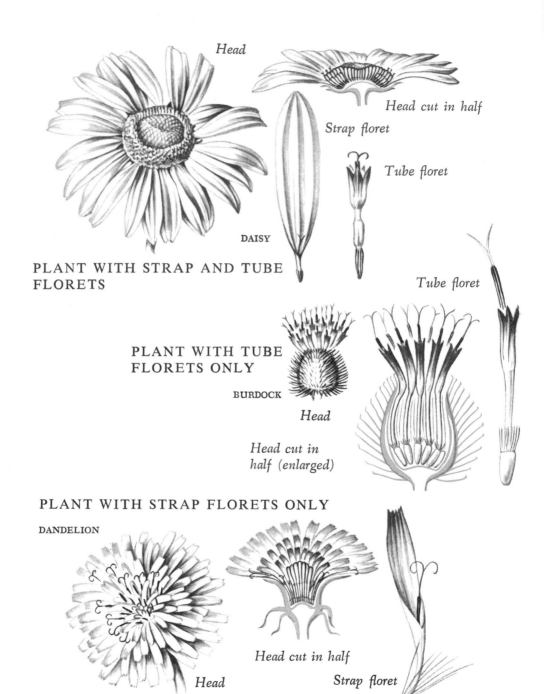

Head

Head cut in half

Strap floret

Tube floret

DAISY

PLANT WITH STRAP AND TUBE FLORETS

Tube floret

PLANT WITH TUBE FLORETS ONLY

BURDOCK

Head

Head cut in
half (enlarged)

PLANT WITH STRAP FLORETS ONLY

DANDELION

Head cut in half

Head

Strap floret

composites are like the sunflower and daisy, with both tubular and strap florets. Some—such as burdock, thistle, boneset—are composed entirely of tube flowers; others—like dandelion and chicory—have only strap flowers.

Nearly all composites are insect pollinated. On page 51 we saw how this is accomplished in a tubular floret. Nectar is produced from a ridge around the base of the style in such quantities that it rises high in the corolla tube. It can be reached even by short-tongued insects. So the flower heads are visited by a great variety of pollinizers. Ragweed and wormwood, however, are wind pollinated.

GENERAL CHARACTERISTICS:

1. The tiny flowers are arranged in compact heads.

2. The calyx is reduced to a few scales or hairs, called the pappus. Occasionally it is cup-shaped or absent.

3. The corolla is five-lobed, either tubular or strap-shaped.

4. There are five stamens, with anthers united into a tube. The filaments are separate.

5. The pistil has a forked stigma, usually with minute hairs on the outside of its branches. The ovary is inferior, with one ovule.

6. The fruits are achenes, usually with special attachments for distribution: parachutes, spines, wings, etc.

4

6

SNEEZEWEED

GALINSOGA

CHAMOMILE

COREOPSIS

STICKSEED

WILD LETTUCE

Index of Plants Referred to in Illustrations and Text

The authority for all Latin names listed here is *The New Britton and Brown Illustrated Flora* by Henry A. Gleason (New York Botanical Garden). However, in accordance with the latest nomenclature, no species designations are capitalized. The abbreviation "spp." (for *species*, plural) indicates that more than one species of a genus is referred to. Common names are hyphenated when the adjective is an invariable part of the name: red-clover, fringed-gentian. Some plants included in the text are omitted from this list: plants familiar to everyone, such as well-known garden plants, and very exotic plants which are merely mentioned.

114

Candytuft, *Iberis* spp., 92, 94
Carolina-jessamine, *Gelsemium sempervirens*, 58
Carrion-flower, *Smilax herbacea*, 29
Carrot, *Daucus carota*, 78, 105
Castor-bean, *Ricinus communis*, 17
Catalpa, *Catalpa speciosa*, 59
Celandine, *Chelidonium majus*, 50
Chamomile, *Matricaria chamomilla*, 113
Cherry, *Prunus cerasus*, 95, 98
Chicory, *Cichorium intybus*, 3, 110, 113
Christmas-rose, *Helleborus niger*, 62, 89
Cinquefoil, *Potentilla* spp., 97; *P. simplex*, 96
Citron, *Citrus medica*, 50
Clary-sage, *Salvia sclarea*, 25
Clematis, *Clematis paniculata*, 90
Closed-gentian, *Gentiana clausa*, 26
Clover, *Trifolium* spp., 13, 63, 65, 67, 68, 78, 100
Cocklebur, *Xanthium* spp., 73
Colt's-foot, *Tussilago farfara*, 110
Columbine, *Aquilegia* spp., 20, 57, 89; *A. caerulea*, 21
Coral-root, *Corallorhiza* spp., 87
Cow-parsnip, *Heracleum lanatum*, 105, 106
Cuckoo-pint, *Arum maculatum*, 29
Curly-dock, *Rumex crispus*, 47

Daffodil, *Narcissus pseudo-narcissus*, 58
Daisy, *Chrysanthemum leucanthemum*, 68, 72, 73, 112, 113
Dandelion, *Taraxacum officinale*, 3, 72, 112, 113
Dogwood, *Cornus florida*, 64
Dutchman's-breeches, *Dicentra cucullaria*, 57

Easter-lily, *Lilium longiflorum*, 40-41
Elderberry, *Sambucus canadensis*, 69
Elecampane, *Inula helenium*, 110
Evening-primrose, *Oenothera biennis*, 60

False-hellebore, *Veratrum viride*, 49, 81
Fennel, *Foeniculum vulgare*, 104, 105
Fire-pink, *Silene virginica*, 27
Firethorn, *Pyracantha* spp., 95
Fireweed, *Epilobium angustifolium*, 15
Fleabane, *Erigeron* spp., 110
Fool's-parsley, *Aethusa cynapium*, 105
Foxglove, *Digitalis purpurea*, 46, 59
Fringed-loosestrife, *Steironema ciliatum*, 67
Fringed-polygala, *Polygala paucifolia*, 34, 57

Galinsoga, *Galinsoga ciliata*, 113
Garden pea, *Pisum sativum*, 100
Garlic, *Allium sativum*, 14, 79
Goats-beard, *Tragopogon* spp., 72
Golden-Alexanders, *Zizia* spp., 105
Golden-pea, *Thermopsis* spp., 100
Goldenrod, *Solidago juncea*, 110, 111
Golden-seal, *Hydrastis canadensis*, 63, 89
Gold-thread, *Coptis trifolia*, 89
Greenbrier, *Smilax* spp., 79
Ground-cherry, *Physalis heterophylla*, 48, 58
Ground-ivy, *Glecoma hederacea*, 107
Ground-nut, *Apios americana*, 100

Hawthorn, *Crataegus* spp., 68, 95, 99; *C. mollis*, 96
Heal-all, *Prunella vulgaris*, 39, 65, 107
Heliotrope, *Heliotropium* spp., 69

115

116

117

Sweet-clover, *Melilotus officinalis*, 100
Sweet-pea, *Lathyrus odoratus*, 50, 100, 101
Sweet-rocket, *Hesperis matronalis*, 92

Tansy, *Tanacetum vulgare*, 110
Thistle, *Cirsium* spp., 110
Tick-trefoil, *Desmodium* spp., 57, 100, 103
Tiger-lily, *Lilium tigrinum*, 66
Timothy, *Phleum pratense*, 38
Toadflax, *Linaria vulgaris*, 26
Toothwort, *Dentaria laciniata*, 43
Trillium, *Trillium* spp., 43, 79
Trout-lily, *Erythronium* spp., 62, 81
Tulip, *Tulipa* spp., 7, 79
Turtlehead, *Chelone glabra*, 26

Vanilla, *Vanilla planifolia*, 86, 87
Violet, *Viola* spp., 20, 21, 46

Wallflower, *Cheiranthus* spp. and *Erysimum* spp., 92
Walnut, *Juglans* spp., 17, 32
Watercress, *Nasturtium officinale*, 92
Waterlily, *Nymphaea* spp., 49

White-campion, *Lychnis alba*, 64
Wild azalea, *Rhododendron nudiflorum*, 49
Wild cherry, *Prunus serotina*, 7, 95, 98
Wild geranium, *Geranium maculatum*, 3, 8-12, 42, 45, 56, 61, 77
Wild ginger, *Asarum canadense*, 61
Wild leek, *Allium tricoccum*, 80
Wild lettuce, *Lactuca canadensis*, 113
Wild rose, *Rosa virginiana*, 56, 62, 95
Wild strawberry, *Fragaria virginiana*, 98
Wintercress, *Barbarea vulgaris*, 92
Wintergreen, *Gaultheria procumbens*, 58
Wood-anemone, *Anemone quinquefolia*, 44
Woody-nightshade, *Solanum dulcamara*, 53
Wormwood, *Artemisia vulgaris*, 110, 111, 113

Yarrow, *Achillea millefolium*, 68, 110
Yucca, *Yucca* spp., 51

Index

119